The Christmas Book

Everything you want to know about the festival of Christmas is in this book: how to appreciate its history and traditions; how to prepare for and enjoy it; and how to recover from it!

Renowned as a home entertainer Gyles Brandreth has amusing suggestions for party games, carols and Christmas readings, with helpful advice on staging nativity plays and pantomimes at home. He has plenty of practical suggestions too on planning a catering calendar (with recipes), making cards and decorations and selecting (and disposing of) presents.

And if you want more than a traditional English Christmas his survey of customs world-wide will give you plenty of new ideas.

* Christmas traditions
* Countdown to December 25th
* Cards and decorations
* Festive food
* Present ideas
* Carols – words and music
* Christmas readings
* Plays and pantomimes
* Games

Illustrated
by
SUE SCULLARD

ROBERT HALE · LONDON

THE CHRISTMAS BOOK

GYLES BRANDRETH

© Gyles Brandreth 1984
First published in Great Britain 1984
First paperback edition 1985
Reprinted 1986

Robert Hale Limited
Clerkenwell House
Clerkenwell Green
London EC1R 0HT

British Library Cataloguing in Publication Data

Brandreth, Gyles
  The Christmas book.
  1. Christmas.
  I. Title
  394.2'68282   GT4985

  ISBN 0-7090-2388-X

Photoset in North Wales by
Derek Doyle & Associates, Mold, Clwyd.
Printed in Great Britain by
St Edmundsbury Press Ltd, Bury St Edmunds, Suffolk.
Bound by Woolnough Bookbinders Limited.

Contents

The First Noel

Christmas is special. Christmas is magic. It is a time of warmth and peace. A season when we can revel unashamedly in nostalgia and tradition. The cynics amongst us have described Christmas as a period of preparations, invitations, anticipations, relations, frustrations, prostration and recuperation! But to most of us it is, above all else, a time of celebration. It always has been, and let's hope it always will be.

In the Christian world Christmas is celebrated in remembrance of the birth of Christ. It is literally the 'Mass of Christ'. Yet, strangely, the rituals associated with this religious festival are of pagan origin and were celebrated long before Christ was born.

Since time immemorial it has been in Man's nature to worship *something*, and because all life seems so dependent on that burning ball of fire in the sky, so vital to the success of harvests, early man went down on his knees and prayed to the sun. In the winter, the strength of the sun being less, it became necessary to slaughter animals for food, and these became the first religious sacrifices. In December, the annual rebirth of the sun turned into an important festival, and many traditions and rituals became established. In Rome on 25 December the *Dies Natalis Invicti Solis* was celebrated – the Birthday of the Unconquered Sun – sacred to Mithras, the god of light, and to Attis, the Phrygian sun god.

The festival was known as the Saturnalia and was a period of celebrations from 17 December right through to the New Year (Kalends) when the Latins rejoiced that the days were getting longer and the power of the sun stronger. It was a time of real merrymaking, when bonfires were lit, homes were decorated with special greenery, people gave each other presents, and there were lots of fun and games. Not blowing up balloons and playing video games, but an early form of charades in which slaves dressed up as their masters, and lords pretended to be servants, and it is said that people danced through the streets wearing very little but blackened faces and a smile!

These pre-Christian celebrations didn't just take place in Ancient Rome, for at the same time in Europe the winter solstice, when the sun is farthest from the equator and at the point when it appears to be returning, became known as the Festival of Yule. In Britain, France (Gaul), Germany, Denmark, Sweden and especially Norway, the Yule or 'Juul' celebrations became the highlight of the year. Yule logs and candles were lit to the gods Odin and Thor,

8

houses were decorated with evergreens, Yule food and drink were prepared, and mistletoe was ceremoniously cut. Although over two thousand years old, the Yule traditions are still continued today.

In Britain the Druids celebrated the Festival of Nolagh, and it is thought by some that Stonehenge was built as a temple to the sun, constructed in such a way that it cast shadows wherever the sun happened to be. In fact, practically every country in the world, from China to India, from South America to the Middle East, held celebrations at this time of year. In Greece it was the birthday of Hercules, Ceres and Bacchus (an excuse to indulge in the grape); the Egyptians claimed it as the feast day of Horus; it was not until the fourth century that Pope Julius I decided that 25 December should be celebrated as the birthday of Jesus Christ, and Christmas as we know it began.

We now celebrate Christmas every year, but with a little bit of pagan tradition, a Norse Yule log, Druid candles, a drop of wine from Saturnalia, and a feast from the winter solstice. The evergreens and mistletoe still decorate our homes, and each year we continue to give presents to those we love. That's the magic of Christmas.

Advent

Advent begins on 1 December and marks the period leading up to Christmas. Children make Advent calendars, a custom which originated in Germany at the end of the nineteenth century. A large calendar was constructed which had twenty-four tiny doors, one of which was opened by the children on each day of December leading up to Christmas Eve, and inside was a small present or chocolate. Today, Advent calendars have a little picture for each day, the final one being a Nativity scene, of course.

In pre-Reformation days Advent models of the Virgin Mary and the baby Jesus, of the kind seen now in a church crib at Christmas, were taken round to every house. Householders paid the church one halfpenny at this time and were said to have luck for the next twelve months. It was thought to be extremely unlucky if you did not see an Advent model before Christmas. This custom was abolished by Henry VIII.

In Germany a customary decoration for Advent is a wreath made from pine branches and suspended from the ceiling by ribbons. It has four candles on it, one of which is lit on each

Sunday in Advent so that by the fourth Sunday, the one prior to Christmas, all candles have been lit. This pagan ritual of lighting candles was thought to ward off evil spirits. A sweet yeast bread called *Christstollen* is also baked during Advent, which is covered in white icing and made to look like the babe wrapped in swaddling clothes.

St Barbara's Day

4 December is St Barbara's Day and has been celebrated in European countries since the twelfth century. Legend says that St Barbara was executed because of her strong belief in Christianity. She is the patron saint of miners, and a light is burnt in mines in her honour, which is said to protect them. On this day 'Barbara twigs' are cut, which usually bloom in time for Christmas.

St Nicholas' Day

The Feast of St Nicholas is 6 December, and this is traditionally when the Christmas season begins, although by this time shops have usually been filled with cards and decorations for months! Little is known about St Nicholas, except that he was the Bishop of Myra in Lycia in Asia Minor some sixteen hundred years ago. There are several stories associated with him, and they quite naturally nearly all concern children.

One says that a father had three young daughters but was so poor that he had no money for dowries, which meant that they could not marry. The father decided that his daughters would have to become 'ladies of the night' and earn some money through the world's oldest profession. Fortunately for them, St Nicholas heard of their plight and threw three bags of gold through their bedroom window one night and so saved them from a fate worse than death. The girls were able to marry, and for his trouble St Nick became the patron saint of prostitutes!

Another story says that a rich nobleman decided to send his three sons to Athens to be educated. They reached Myra, where St Nicholas was bishop, and had to stay the night at an inn. The innkeeper, seeing that the boys were rich, murdered them in the night for their money and chopped up their bodies, which he placed in a large pot with some pork that was being pickled. St Nicholas had a vision of what had happened, rushed to the inn and accused the innkeeper of the crime. Immediately the innkeeper confessed and showed where the bodies were. St Nicholas prayed for help and brought the children back to life. There used to be a custom of electing a boy bishop to take the services in cathedrals from St Nicholas' Day until Holy Innocents Day (28 December). If the boy died during this period he was buried with the full honours of a bishop, and in Salisbury Cathedral there is a monument to a boy bishop who died 'in office'. The custom was a direct result of this story.

It is as Santa Claus that we now know St Nicholas, the patron saint of children, and in Britain and America we have amalgamated St Nicholas' Day with Christmas Day and so give presents on 25 December, rather than 6 December. In many Catholic countries, though, children still hang up their stockings on St Nicholas' Eve.

In Germany and Switzerland St Nicholas sometimes arrives wearing a bishop's outfit, but more usually he is dressed in the familiar red and white tunic of Santa Claus. Unlike the kindly old man whom we expect, St Nicholas is also carrying a book of sins and can punish naughty children as well as give presents to the good. This no doubt encourages children to be good at this time! He is accompanied by a fierce henchman called 'Black Peter' who will haunt the dreams of naughty children. To get into St Nicholas' good books, children leave a bowl of water and a carrot outside for his horse.

In some countries St Nicholas and Santa Claus (or Sinte Klaas, as he is known in Holland) are two different people, in others they are one and the same. In Germany many children are luckier than most because they receive presents from St Nicholas on the 6th *and* from Santa Claus on 24 December! In France children leave little wooden clogs on their hearth and believe that it is the Christ Child himself who brings their gifts.

St Lucia's Day

On 13 December St Lucia's Day (occasionally known as 'Little Yule') is celebrated in Sweden and is a festival left over from the old winter solstice days. The real Lucia was a fourth-century martyr and appears to have little to do with the festivals associated with her. Every year each village in Sweden elects a 'Lucia Queen', who on this day has to dress in white and wear a crown of lighted candles on her head. Despite the havoc dripping candlewax must have on her hairstyle, the girl carries trays of food and drink to each house in the village, followed by a procession of candlebearers, symbolizing the returning strength of the sun.

St Thomas's Day

21 December is the winter solstice and known as St Thomas's Day, some feel because 'doubting Thomas' should be remembered on the longest night of the year. In past days this was the favourite time for giving money to charities. At Bolingbroke in Lincolnshire the vicar holds a special 'candle auction', during which he sticks a pin in a lighted candle and accepts bids for the grazing rights on a piece of land let for charity. The last bid received before the pin falls decides who will be the tenant and how much he will have to pay for the coming year.

St Thomas's Day used to be a school holiday, too. Not out of any particular respect for St Thomas, but because of a 'barring out' custom, (practised all over England) which meant that children could arrive at school early and barricade the teachers out! Because no teachers could get in, it was naturally declared a holiday!

'Thomassing' was another custom which took place on this particular day, when people from poorer families could go and knock on the doors of richer households and beg flour with which to make Christmas bread and cakes. It was sometimes known as 'going a-corning' because they were occasionally given wheat with which to make their own flour.

For a girl wishing to know what her future husband will look like, an ancient superstition says that if she sleeps with her feet on the pillow on St Thomas's Eve, she will dream of the man she will marry. Presumably she prays first that it will not be a nightmare!

Christmas Eve

24 December is the time of real anticipation as far as children are concerned, and a time of last-minute preparation for mothers and fathers. Traditionalists say that you can put up your Christmas decorations and cards any time after 6 December, but purists maintain that you may only start to festoon your home on Christmas Eve.

In pre-central-heating days an important task on Christmas Eve was that of bringing in the Yule log to burn in the grate over the festive period. Traditionally it was lit with a piece of the previous year's Yule log for luck. In many homes today a Yule candle is lit instead, but it must burn the whole night through to avoid bad luck throughout the coming year.

An ancient English custom claims that a loaf of bread baked on Christmas Eve will have all kinds of curative powers. Just one slice of it is said to stop diarrhoea, dysentery and all kinds of related ills. Considering the variety of rich food you are likely to over-indulge in at this time, a slice of this bread would be no bad thing! According to an ancient Oxfordshire custom, if a single girl bakes a loaf on Christmas Eve, it will help her discover the identity of her husband-to-be. She has got to fast throughout the day (a pre-Christmas diet!), call the loaf she bakes a 'Dumb Cake' and prick it with her initials before leaving it by the hearth and retiring to bed. At the stroke of midnight, her future groom's double will enter the room, leave his initials next to hers and depart. However, he'll only come if the girl has remembered to leave the front door ajar. If the door isn't open at midnight, the girl will be condemned to a life of spinsterhood. If she leaves the door open, however, she might be condemned to something else!

Remarkable occurrences are said to take place on Christmas Eve. During it all sorts of extraordinary things are believed to happen. If you visit a farm, you will discover that it is like a reincarnation of George Orwell's *Animal Farm*, for animals will have the power of speech, and bees hum the Hundredth Psalm at midnight. On second thoughts, don't go too near the cowshed or pigsty, for if you do eavesdrop on them, dire things will happen to you.

An early death is the fate of all who want to listen to the angels sing on Christmas Eve. You'll be able to hear them by sitting under a pine tree: the music's sweet, but the price is dear. Perhaps it is only shepherds on the hillside who have the privilege. There is no penalty, however, for listening to cocks crowing on Christmas Eve. They all do it – even weathercocks – because it was a cock that first proclaimed the birth of Jesus by crowing *'Christus Natus Est'* on the night of the first Christmas.

In Norway, Finland and Denmark you will find that traditional Christmas fare is sucking-pig, followed by *Reisbrei*, a kind of milk pudding with cinnamon and melted butter on the top. In many European countries Christmas Eve is the time for eating the main Christmas meal, although in Catholic countries it is a time of fasting, and they wait until Christmas Day to feast. In areas of Germany, around the Black Forest, an extra place is laid at the table

13

for the Virgin Mary. Not that they expect her to come, but it makes up for the fact that there was no room for her in Bethlehem.

Whatever their religion, many people go to church for Midnight Mass, and one thing you will certainly hear is Christmas bells, which are rung throughout the land. The most famous traditional bell-ringing ceremony is the tolling of the Devil's Knell which begins at 11 p.m. on 24 December at Dewsbury in Yorkshire. The knell is pulled for the same number of times as years which have elapsed since the birth of Christ.

Your final duty on Christmas Eve should be to hang up your Christmas stocking for Santa to fill. Nobody really knows why we hang a stocking, but legend has it that when the athletic bishop St Nicholas threw the three bags of gold to the virgins, the gold landed in their stockings hanging by the fire to dry! Presumably he threw it down the chimney!

Christmas Day

The climax of the Christmas season is, of course, 25 December, the First Day of Christmas. A very special day for family and friends, a time of exchanging gifts, for enjoying good food and wine, and if you are a Christian a time for going to church to celebrate the birth of Jesus.

More than any other day in the year, Christmas Day is one of tradition. A day of traditional food, for although we rarely eat the boar's head, roast swan, capons, peacocks or venison of bygone days, our Christmas dinner of turkey or goose, plum pudding and mince pies has a long history.

The first Christmas pudding was a kind of broth, to which raisins, spices and breadcrumbs were added, plus a drop of wine or ale. Two hundred years ago the mixture was boiled in a cloth. It was the Victorians, of course, who thought of the delightful idea of placing lucky charms and silver threepenny pieces in the pudding. This tradition is still continued, and if nothing else it encourages children to eat the pudding in the hope of finding a little trinket!

Mince pies were first made in Tudor times, although they were then rectangular rather than round as we now bake them. Elizabethan recipes refer to them as 'coffins', probably because that was their shape. A superstition then was that every mince pie you ate would bring you one month of luck in the year ahead, so you had to eat at least twelve. That's a good enough excuse to make a pig of yourself.

Naturally there are lots of superstitions and beliefs associated with Christmas Day. Any child born on this day, apart from being landed with the name Noel or Noelle, is said to have the gift of genius, and psychic powers too. Sir Isaac Newton, for example, was born on Christmas Day 1642. They will have the disadvantage of receiving joint Christmas/birthday cards and presents though. Every genius has to pay the price!

We've all got fairies at the bottom of our gardens (or window boxes!) and they must not be forgotten on Christmas Day if you want good fortune. While you are out walking off that last slice of Christmas pudding, clearing your head from your third tot of sherry, picking up Auntie Winnie and Cousin Beatrice from church, or visiting the neighbours to collect your Christmas present, the fairies will visit your house to give it the once-over. If they discover your house beautifully neat and tidy, with a splendid array of food, they will make sure you have a good time in the year ahead. If it is dirty and dusty, with a sink full of washing-up and the beds unmade, you will suffer for it in the months to come. Hopefully the fairies will forgive a few bits of Christmas wrapping-paper left scattered around the children's bedroom!

The weather on Christmas Day is also significant to the coming year for it foretells what will happen. Thomas Passenger, a seventeenth-century weather forecaster and author of that best-selling tome the *Shepherd's Kalendar*, wrote: 'If the sun shine clear and bright on Christmas Day, it promiseth a peaceable year from clamours and strife and foretells much plenty to ensue; but if the wind blow stormy toward sunset, it betokeneth sickness in the spring and autumn quarters.'

Naturally most people long for a white Christmas, but in Great Britain this generally leads to disappointment. London has known only seven white Christmases since the turn of the century – they were 1906, 1917, 1923, 1927, 1938, 1956 and 1970 – although that didn't stop Bing Crosby's 'White Christmas' becoming a best-selling record, and still popular even though it was first issued in 1941.

Since 1932 a new tradition has evolved. On Christmas Day 1932 King George V spoke to the nation over the air-waves, a tradition that his granddaughter has continued, and all but the most hardened anti-monarchists now include Her Majesty's annual speech as an essential part of Christmas.

Boxing Day

26 December, although popularly known as Boxing Day, is also the Feast of St Stephen, which is when old Good King Wenceslas looked out. St Stephen was the first Christian martyr and was stoned to death for his faith (AD 33). He is connected with horses, and it is because of this association that this day is particularly important for huntsmen, who always ride to the hounds. This has become more of a social gathering than a bloodthirsty fox-hunt. Until recent years horses were actually taken to St Stephen's grave in Norrtalje and were ceremoniously bled. This was thought to ensure good health to the horses, and from all accounts the practice did no harm.

The name 'Boxing Day' comes from the practice on this day of opening the church alms-boxes. The contents were distributed to the poor as the 'dole of the Christmas box'. The tradition was started by the Romans, another old Saturnalia custom, and full alms-boxes were actually unearthed from the ruins of Pompeii, the city devastated by the eruption of Vesuvius in AD 79. The practice continued until the Reformation.

The tradition of giving a sum of money, 'a Christmas box', to people who have been of service throughout the year still persists. Tradesmen, such as milkmen, dustmen, postmen and delivery boys, still expect a tip for Christmas, but as many are on holiday now from Christmas to New Year, few receive their 'Christmas Box' actually on Boxing Day.

In the village of Drayton Beauchamp, Buckinghamshire, for several centuries a custom allowed the villagers to visit the rectory on Boxing Day and demand as much bread, cheese and ale as they could eat. When one rector tried to stop this practice by hiding in his cellar and pretending to be out, the marauding villagers besieged the house and ate and drank everything they could lay their hands on. Fortunately for succeeding rectors, the custom was stopped in 1808.

In many countries, Boxing Day is a day of family reunions and outings, but universally it is a day of recovery, of nursing overblown stomachs and curing hangover headaches!

New Year's Eve

'The King is dead! Long live the King!' 31 December is, of course, the time for ringing out the old year and ringing in the new, and in past centuries this is literally what happened, for bells rang out all over the land.

Although Sassenachs south of the border celebrate the New Year, in Scotland they go to town, for there Hogmanay really supersedes Christmas. The word 'Hogmanay' comes from the Greek *'Hagmena'* which means 'Holy moon' and stems back to those old pagan customs once again. On New Year's Eve the Druids used to go out and cut down mistletoe to hang in their houses to protect them against evil spirits.

The most important tradition associated with New Year today is First Footing. The First Footer is the first person to enter your house after midnight, but if he is to bring good luck with him, there are certain requirements. He must be uninvited and a stranger (advice about not letting strange men into your home goes by the board on New Year's Eve, but keep an eye on the silver!); he must have dark hair and be neither cross-eyed nor flat-footed (whoever heard of a flat-footed First Footer?); and he must be carrying a lump of coal, a slice of bread, a pinch of salt and an evergreen into the house. The dark stranger cannot be a woman, even in these days of sex-equality, for this brings bad luck to the house.

Women need not feel left out, however, for they must polish the house (especially the silver) to make a clean start to the new year, but must not dust or vacuum until after midday on 1 January, otherwise they could accidentally sweep up their quota of good luck!

Although the Scots may go overboard at New Year and First Foot all night long, the rest of the world have their little traditions too, of course. In the Channel Islands a mock figure of Old Father Time is buried in the sand to symbolize the burying of the old year. In Wales young men from the villages sprinkle people with fresh spring water to bring them luck. Czechoslovakians leave one window open and one closed, to let out the old and in the new. In Bavaria coins are tied around trees with ribbon to make them more fruitful, and in parts of Germany the New Year is 'blown' in by

17

trombonists, and an annual custom is to drop molten lead into cold water: the shapes that the lead makes are interpreted to show what the New Year has in store, rather like reading tea-leaves.

Amongst the New Year festivities in Britain, the oldest at this time of year is 'wassailing'. Wassail songs were sung to drive evil spirits away in the past. Wassailers also carried with them a wooden bowl containing a kind of punch made from warm ale, apples, sugar and spices. People would pay a few pence to drink from the wassail bowl when the wassailers called at their house, rather like carol singers today. Many wassail songs still exist, apart from the most famous of all, 'Here we come a-wassailing'. One of the oldest goes:

> Good master, at your door,
> Our wassail we begin;
> We all are maidens poor,
> So we pray you let us in
> And drink our wassail.

In pagan times wassail songs were sung to fruit trees, and punch from the wassail bowl was poured over the tree roots to ensure a good harvest.

At a few minutes to midnight, wherever you are, you should make your New Year resolutions, resolving not to break them! Then at the stroke of midnight, join hands with your family and friends to sing the most popular New Year song of all:

> Should auld acquaintance be forgot,
> And never brought to min'?
> Should auld acquaintance be forgot,
> And days o'lang syne?
>
> We twa hae rin about the braes,
> And put the gowans fine;
> But we've wander'd monie a weary fit
> Sin' auld lang syne.
>
> We twa hae paid'lt i' the burn,
> Frae mornin' sun till dine;
> But seas between us braid hae roar'd
> Sin' auld lang syne.

And here's a hand, my trusty fiere,
And gie's a hand o'thine;
And we'll tak a right gude-willie-waught
For auld lang syne.

And surely ye'll be your pint-stowp,
And surely I'll be mine;
And we'll tak a cup o'kindness yet
For auld lang syne!

For auld lang syne, my dear,
For auld lang syne,
We'll tak a cup o'kindness yet
For auld lang syne.

Twelfth Night

6 January, the Feast of Epiphany, marks the official end of Christmas. Twelfth Night marks the pilgrimage of the Three Kings to the baby Jesus in Bethlehem, bearing gifts of gold, frankincense and myrrh. In Germany the day is known as *Dreikönigstag*, 'The Three King's Day', and it is not until this day that the figures of the Kings are actually added to the Christmas crib in churches.

Throughout the Christian world a number of special church services take place. The most intriguing of these is held annually in the Chapel Royal of St James's Palace in London, and has been for over nine hundred years. Until the end of the eighteenth century the reigning monarch carried out the ceremony, but now two Gentlemen Ushers of the Royal Household do this on the Queen's behalf and re-enact the Kings' presentations of gold, frankincense and myrrh. Until the time of Queen Victoria gold leaf was used as the gold, but in 1860 this was changed to 25 gold sovereigns, which are now exchanged for present-day currency and given to charity. The frankincense is given to the church, and the myrrh is donated to a hospital.

A less spiritual ceremony, but none the less intriguing, takes place in a different part of London. In the Green Room of the Theatre Royal, Drury Lane, the cast and company of the current show tuck in to a special Twelfth Night cake. It is provided each year out of the interest from £100 bequeathed for the purpose by an actor-cum-chef called Robert Baddeley who died in his dressing-room there in 1794. The cake is eaten in his honour, and is still carried into the dressing-room by attendants in eighteenth-century uniform. It is one cake, however, that you will not get a slice of, unless you happen to be appearing at Drury Lane.

Just as Twelfth Night marked the end of the Three Kings' journey, so it marks the end of our journey from Advent to Epiphany, the official end of the festive season. Decorations can be left in churches until Candlemas (2 February), but they must at all costs be removed from homes by midnight on 6 January. Down must come the tinsel, the holly, the balloons, the Christmas cards, the Christmas tree ...

A new born year is waiting,
To meet the early dawn;
And whisper this to all the world,
Another Christmas gone.

CHRISTMAS
IS COMING

The Twelve Months of Christmas

Every year it's the same. Nineteen shopping days left to Christmas and not a card written, a caked iced or a present bought. Before you know it, you're left with the scraggiest turkey the farmer could rear, send Christmas cards by first-class mail to ensure that they at least arrive by New Year, and end up buying Great Aunt Mona slippers for the sixth year running because you simply haven't the time or the inclination to think of something slightly more original. Yes, come what may, as regular as Christmas itself it's a frantic last-minute panic down to the shops, leaving your nerves and your bank balance severely frayed!

With just a little bit of planning, all this can be avoided, and it really doesn't take very much effort to reach the festive season with cards not only bought but written ready for posting, the present problem all nicely wrapped up, and the menu planned from Christmas Eve to New Year's Day.

In 1747 Lord Chesterfield wrote to his son: 'There is time enough for everything in the course of the day if you do but one thing at once; but there is not time enough in the year if you will do two things at a time.' Words of wisdom indeed, for it is at the festive time of year that we fall flat on our faces by trying to do half-a-dozen things at once, and as a result we get nowhere fast! Because Christmas is such an important part of the year with so much to do, why not spread the load over twelve months? By the time Christmas comes, you'll have enough time to do as much wassailing and merrymaking as you like.

Countdown to Christmas

Here's how to plan your Christmas so that it becomes a time of joy, rather than one of dread.

January

It's never too soon to start planning Christmas, and as anyone who has ever worked in a major department store will know, by January they have planned exactly what their approach to next Christmas will be, from the stock they are going to sell to what their window display will be.

This is not the time for you to start thinking *too* seriously about next Christmas – after all, you've only just recovered from the last one. But some preparation won't go amiss, and the most important thing to do in January is to buy your Christmas cards. This takes a lot of will-power, but forget the excuses like 'Oh, I'll have lost them by December' or 'Well, maybe I'll be able to buy more expensive ones by then' – you won't! Buy them now, while they are cheap. You can usually get very good cards at half the original price or less, when it will quite naturally have doubled in ten months' time.

Having bought them, get a large cardboard box and mark it 'Christmas 19 –'. Keep the box safely in a cupboard, and every time you buy something towards Christmas, simply put it in the box and you'll have everything together when the time comes.

No sooner has Twelfth Night passed and the last vestiges of Christmas have been thrown from your house, than the January sales begin! Bountiful though the bargains may be, this is not the time for major Christmas shopping. The gift chosen for your daughter or husband in January, even though they would give their right arm for it now, will have lost its magic by next December, and they may even buy the very same item in the same sale! It is, nevertheless, an excellent time to stock up on those universal gifts that could be given to anyone at any time, from beautiful silk handkerchiefs to delightfully boxed stationery sets, classic gifts that will be a third of the price in January and out of your price range next December.

February – April

For anyone who likes a drop of the Christmas spirit to see them through the Christmas season, February can be made all the more enjoyable by planning the alcoholic beverages that will see you through the crucial twelve days. When it comes to buying alcoholic liquor at Christmas, the prices can seem very steep, even if it's only a case of buying a bottle of sherry to keep Grandma amused and a tot of brandy for the Christmas pudding.

To avoid the Christmas doldrums, start gathering together your cellar now and take advantage of seasonal special offers over the coming months. Do, however, make sure that anything you buy is placed in a sealed box and not touched for another ten months, or your object will have been defeated!

Better still, make the most of the long February evenings by *making* your own wine. There are lots of easy-to-use wine-making kits on the market which result in excellent wine, or if you can gather together the equipment, you can make your own brews from carrots, potatoes and practically anything else you can lay your hands on! Whatever you make, it will take until Christmas to mature, and if you really have the will-power, start brewing for Christmases in years to come!

An early spring trip to France for the day is an excellent way of gathering together a reasonably priced stock of duty-free wines and spirits. A bargain-priced day-trip will more than pay for itself on the amount you will be able to bring back with you.

During half-term and the Easter holidays, children can be kept occupied inventing new games that all the family can play. Anything that they develop with an Easter theme can easily be adapted to suit Christmas too.

May – June

If you have a deep-freeze, now and through the summer is the period to start thinking of putting fruit and vegetables by for your Christmas menus. Choose vegetables especially that will not be freshly available in December. Asparagus, for example, freezes perfectly (and having been frozen takes very little time to cook) and would be a splendid accompaniment to your Christmas dinner. Strawberries never freeze well, but raspberries and loganberries do and make an excellent light dessert on Boxing Day after the heavy puddings, cakes and pastry that have preceded it. Gooseberries are ideal for freezing, and a light gooseberry fool would be perfect after a heavy main course and a delightful change at Christmas. This is a splendid time for making jams and preserves to consume during the winter months too. There is nothing like the taste of summer during the cold days of winter.

July – August

This is the time to begin thinking seriously about Christmas presents. At this time most of the large shops and department stores hold their summer sales, and this provides an excellent opportunity for the Christmas shopper to get the headache of present-buying over and done with once and for all. The reason for the sales is, of course, that the shops (like you!) are preparing for Christmas, and as soon as the sales are ended in September, they will be filled with tinsel and bunting, and Christmas shopping will begin in earnest. You will have beaten them to it by doing your present shopping during, rather than after, the sales!

During the sales practically *everything* is reduced in price, from perfumes to jewellery, from books to footballs, tape recorders to televisions, so whether it's a fur coat for your film star fiancé or a feather duster for your favourite fifth cousin, take advantage of this heaven-sent opportunity.

Whilst you are soaking up the sun on your summer vacation, the last thing on your mind is likely to be Christmas! No one really expects you to spend your fortnight in Florence or two weeks in Tenerife Christmas shopping, but if you are abroad, take a look at the local industries and unusual curiosities that are produced. For the present that is 'different', nothing could be better than that special gift that you have actually brought from foreign climes; whether it's a genuine boomerang for nephew Nigel or a hand-embroidered tablecloth for Aunt Millicent, it is certain to be a gift that is appreciated. Buy a barometer when you visit Japan, and they'll know when it's raining in Yokohama! An unusual present precludes any fears that you give something that the recipient has already got!

September

As the autumn approaches, it is an excellent time to make mincemeat for your mince pies. You can easily buy a jar from the local supermarket, but nothing can ever taste quite like the real thing. Christmas is a time of tradition, and one of the earliest surviving recipes for mincemeat is one created by Sir Kenelme Digbie in 1669, which has the delicious flavour of olde England. The book in which it appeared was given the delightful title of *The Closet of the Eminently Learned Sir Kenelme Digbie Knight, Opened*. Obviously a best-seller in the seventeenth century, it was eventually reprinted in 1910! From Sir Kenelme's closet comes this delicious recipe:

1 cooked calf's tongue (finely chopped)
½ lb of grated suet
4 oz of raisins
½ lb of finely chopped apples
2 oz of candied orange peel
2 oz of candied lemon

4 tablespoons of sherry
Grated rind of one lemon
1 teaspoon of nutmeg
1 teaspoon of mace
$\frac{1}{2}$ teaspoon of cloves
2 teaspoons of cinnamon
4 oz of sugar

Simply mix all the ingredients together in a large bowl and stir them together so that they are well blended, then place in screw-top jars. Keep for at least a month before using, preferably in the refrigerator. It will keep up to Christmas and beyond.

October

With your mincemeat maturing nicely in the fridge, October is the ideal time to make your Christmas cake. Again it is simple to buy one, but making your own is not difficult, and it tastes altogether different. Really good Christmas cake improves with keeping, which is why you should make it by the end of October. Wrap it in tinfoil and put it in an air-tight tin and it will keep perfectly. Many people keep a small piece of their cake from one Christmas to the next without any problems.

You will find the recipe for a traditional iced Christmas cake in Chapter 4, but for the taste of a bygone age here is how the great Mrs Beeton did it in 1861:

5 cupfuls of flour
1 teacupful of melted butter
1 teacupful of cream
$\frac{1}{2}$ teacupful of treacle
1 teacupful of moist sugar
2 eggs
$\frac{1}{2}$ oz of powdered ginger
$\frac{1}{2}$ lb of raisins
1 teaspoonful of bicarbonate of soda
1 tablespoonful of vinegar

Make the butter sufficiently warm to melt it, but do not allow it to oil; put the flour into a basin, add to it the sugar, ginger and raisins, which should be cut into small pieces. When these dry ingredients are thoroughly mixed, stir in the butter, cream, treacle and well-whisked eggs, and beat the mixture for a few minutes. Mix the soda with the dry ingredients, being very careful to leave no lumps, and stir the vinegar into the dough. When it is wetted, put the cake into a buttered mould or tin, place it in a moderate oven immediately and bake it from $1\frac{3}{4}$ hours to $2\frac{1}{4}$ hours.

Strangely, Mrs Beeton's cake is not a good keeper and should be made only a couple of weeks before Christmas if this is the recipe you intend to use. To make it last longer, turn the cake over and prick the base. Then pour a little sherry or brandy over it.

November

The Sunday nearest the Feast of St Andrew (30 November) is known as Stir Sunday. It gets its name from the collect for the day, 'Stir up, we beseech Thee, O Lord, the wills of thy faithful people.' On Stir Sunday you are traditionally meant to make your Christmas pudding. Here is the recipe for an Edwardian favourite (you will find another traditional recipe in Chapter 4):

12 oz of raisins
6 oz of currants
6 oz of sultanas
8 oz of brown sugar
$\frac{1}{2}$ teaspoon of mixed spice
1 oz of ground almonds
Grated rind of one lemon
$\frac{1}{4}$ grated nutmeg
4 eggs
3 oz of glacé cherries (chopped)
3 oz of mixed peel
4 oz of flour
8 oz of breadcrumbs
8 oz of suet
Pinch of salt
Brandy

Place all the dry ingredients in a bowl, gradually stir in the beaten eggs and sufficient brandy to make a moist mixture. Place in a greased bowl and cover with a pudding cloth. Steam for seven to eight hours. The pudding will keep for several months but should be steamed for another two to three hours before serving.

While the Christmas pudding is steaming away (don't forget to keep topping up the water so that it doesn't boil dry), you will have plenty of time to prepare your Christmas card list. The ideal method is to make a list like this:

CHRISTMAS CARD LIST

Name	19		19		19		19	
	From	To	From	To	From	To	From	To

Having made your card list, you can use it year after year, and see at a glance whom you need to send cards to, whom you can cross off because they didn't send you one last year, who has passed on or is no longer on speaking terms with you, and no doubt each year your list will be extended to include new-found friends and colleagues who will need a card. Keep the list safely with your Christmas cards and it will be to hand whenever you want it.

Finally, in November buy any wrapping-paper, ribbons, gift-tags and sellotape that you will need before they are unobtainable in a few weeks' time! Buy calendars for the coming new year, too, before all the best have gone. Many people don't consider buying a new one until the New Year is fast approaching, and by then it is too late.

December
1st
Order your Christmas turkey, goose or capons. To ensure that you have a leg of beef on Boxing Day and a joint of pork for New Year,

do your Christmas ordering early in the month to ensure that you have good-quality meat.

2nd
Check the final date by which you need to send cards to friends and relatives overseas.

3rd
Write your Christmas cards. This can be a long, laborious task writing out cards and envelopes, but get it done early in the month and they'll be ready to post later in the month and will be certain to arrive on time.

4th
Write any letters necessary to accompany the cards. Christmas is often the only occasion on which you keep in contact with certain people, the time when you catch up on the news over the past year. If you find that you need to write hundreds, then write one long general newsy letter explaining all the major events and then photocopy it. It may not be as personal, but if you apologize for your newsletter and say that it simply was not possible to write to everyone, people will understand. If you sign it and write a couple of individual lines at the bottom, such as 'Hope we will be able to get to see each other in the New Year', it will be quite acceptable, and people will get to look forward to receiving your annual newsletter.

5th
Prepare any food that can be made in advance and frozen. If you have parties planned, it is a good idea to make fruit flans, quiches, lasagne, dips, pies, sausage rolls, anything that can be frozen for the future. This will save a lot of time nearer Christmas. You can even make your forcemeat and stuffings for Christmas Day and freeze them.

6th
Post any Christmas presents and packages to people whom you will not be seeing before Christmas. These can be sent by second-class mail and will arrive in plenty of time for Christmas. Include your Christmas card and newsletter in the parcel too.

7th
Buy those little extras that are always needed over Christmas but

are often difficult to get when you remember them at the last minute. Icing sugar for your Christmas cake, cranberry sauce to accompany the turkey, paper serviettes if necessary for your parties, candles to light the table, and so on.

8th
Make sure that you have extra provisions to cover the Christmas period. An extra jar of coffee, more butter, some tinned fruit for emergency gate-crashing guests, anything that will keep until Christmas and beyond, that will not spoil if it isn't used but will give you confidence to have it in stock.

9th
Post your Christmas cards. As the Christmas rush begins, post your cards by second-class mail (look for special offers from the Post Office on books of Christmas stamps) to ensure that they will arrive over the coming week. This will jog anyone's memory if they have accidentally missed *you* off their list!

Put the marzipan or almond paste on your Christmas cake.

10th
Ice your Christmas cake. This will give the icing plenty of time to set before you cut the cake on Christmas Day. With any excess icing, make little sweets by adding chocolate powder or peppermint essence. It's often worth making just a little extra so that you can actually make some – they are always popular. Any additional marzipan can be pushed inside dates to produce stuffed dates. A little box of sweets and stuffed dates can be quite an acceptable gift for a neighbour, the newspaper boy, the old man who helps you with the garden, especially if presented attractively in a box.

11th
Wrap your Christmas presents. This can be a tiresome task if you are not particularly artistic, but fun if you set aside an evening with a glass of sherry, a mince pie and carols on the hi-fi to get you in the mood. Make the job easier by writing out a label for each person you have bought a present for. Lay out the presents with a label for each. It is then simply a case of wrapping the present and sticking on the labels as you go.

12th

You will now be in a really festive mood, so begin gathering together your Christmas decorations. If you live in the country, look out for holly and mistletoe, and visit the local farmer with a Christmas box if it happens to be growing on his land. It may be the season of peace and goodwill, but trespassers are not likely to be forgiven. Dust off your old baubles and dig out the tinsel, before turning to Chapter 3 for ideas for new decorations.

13th

Having made your decorations, you can now transform your home into a fantasy of festoons and bunting to put your household into a Christmas spirit. Don't forget the exterior of your house, though. Give it a little colour with a Christmas wreath on the door.

14th

Your final, and possibly one of the most important, decorations must be your Christmas tree. There are many excellent artificial trees available that look so realistic they are often difficult to distinguish from the real thing, but you might wish to have a real one. Useful though artificial trees may be, nothing can replace that wonderful pine aroma that a real tree gives off. When you buy your tree, make sure that it has roots. Not only will you be able to plant the tree later, but you will have less trouble with falling pine needles too. Buy a small tree and put it in a large tub of earth. Place a few stones in the bottom first to give good drainage, and make certain that the tree is watered whilst in the house over Christmas. On Twelfth Night, after you have removed the tree decorations, stand the tub outside. The tree should grow quite happily and can be brought back into the house next Christmas. If you give the tree 'plant food' during the spring and keep the soil moist during hot summer months, it should survive.

15th

Make your first batch of mince pies. If possible make a large enough number to see you through the Christmas period, and freeze. You can take out as few or as many pies as you wish over the coming weeks, and if warmed for ten minutes in the oven, they taste like freshly baked pies.

16th

Place an order with your milkman for extra milk, cream and eggs over the Christmas period. There will be no deliveries for several days, especially if Christmas happens to fall at a weekend, so be sure of a good supply of dairy products. Most milkmen supply soft drinks at this time of year, which will relieve you of one more task.

17th

Go carol singing! Choose a charity that you would like to donate money to, and if you approach them first, they will be quite happy to give you a collecting tin. Form yourself into as large a group as possible, with friends and especially children. There are a few golden rules about the art of carol singing that should be adhered to:

1. Make sure you all know the words and the tunes of the carols you intend to sing. Practise beforehand. A small, well-rehearsed repertoire is better than attempting to sing every carol ever written.
2. Give value for money and allow each house to hear at least one carol all the way through. However, don't labour the point by giving a complete concert!
3. Ring each doorbell only once. Even if you *know* that the occupants are hiding behind the curtain, don't knock the door down.
4. Always appear grateful for the money put in your collecting tin, even if it is only 3p. Don't stop mid-carol or take the money and run!
5. Avoid the temptation to go into people's homes, even if invited. The offer of a warm mince pie and a hot toddy may sound tempting, but it's not the object of the exercise.
6. Wrap up warm and enjoy yourself.

If you collect money for charity, do see that the money reaches its intended destination. This is, after all, the season of goodwill ...

18th

Buy any extra wines and spirits that might be needed for your Christmas parties. Don't forget those extras, like cocktail cherries and sticks, lemons (which will keep for weeks in the fridge wrapped in tinfoil), tonic waters and so on.

19th

Make Christmas crackers and table decorations for your Christmas dinner table. A simple but attractive centrepiece can be created using a piece of florist's 'oasis', into which you can push some candles, the long thin variety, some sprigs of holly complete with berries, and some small twigs sprayed with gold paint or dipped in glitter. During the meal the candles can be lit.

20th

Time for very last-minute Christmas shopping for your nearest and dearest, whose present you don't want to be discovered! By now you should, of course, have got all your presents safely wrapped, but for any small item that you've forgotten, this is the day to get it.

21st

Make the brandy butter for your Christmas pudding. You will need

$\frac{1}{2}$ lb of unsalted butter

6 oz of soft brown sugar

2 teaspoons of grated lemon rind

1 teaspoon of lemon juice

2 tablespoons of brandy

Cream together the butter and sugar. It helps if the butter has been left in a warm room for a couple of hours before you do this. Mix in the lemon rind and lemon juice. Some people prefer the taste of orange rind and orange juice, especially if you are using Grand Marnier. Finally, add the brandy a little at a time, beating the mixture all the time. Put the butter in a dish and cover with tinfoil and store in the refrigerator until Christmas Day.

22nd

Visit a Christmas market and buy the fresh fruits, nuts etc. that are nice to have around. Oranges, tangerines and apples are in plentiful supply, so treat yourself! Do any last minute food shopping.

23rd

If you've ordered a turkey from a local farm or supplier, make sure you collect it or have it delivered by today. If you have frozen a large turkey, get it out of the deep freeze this evening to give it plenty of time to defrost.

24th

Make your forcemeat if you haven't already done so. If you have the kind of oven that can be set by a timer, stuff your turkey and place it in the oven ready to come on early in the morning. This is necessary if it is a very large bird and is going to need many hours' cooking. If you are feeling particularly energetic, you can prepare your vegetables and leave them in saucepans covered with cold salted water. If you lay the table ready for Christmas dinner *before* you go to bed, you can have a nice relaxing Christmas morning opening your presents whilst the dinner cooks itself.

Take any mincepies etc. out of the deep freeze, ready for tomorrow.

Hang up your Christmas stocking!

Party Planning

If you intend to give a party at some time over Christmas or New Year, it is essential to organize it properly if it is to be a success. If the dog turns out to be the life and soul of your parties, you're obviously going wrong somewhere!

If you want to be the hostess with the mostess and not the crème de la crumb, here are a few tips to help make your party a swinging success!

1. Decide what type of party you are going to have.

Is it going to be a fancy dress party with the Gay Nineties as the theme, a quiet dinner party for eight, or a wild disco for teenagers to bop the night away?

2. Draw up a guest list.

For any party to be a success there needs to be a good mix, but choose your guests with care. If it is going to be a lively party for mostly under twenty-fives, don't invite the elderly Joneses from next door who will feel uncomfortable. Invite them round for a quiet dinner one other evening. Likewise, if there are only one or two youngsters in your family, invite a few of their friends so that they have someone of their own age group to join them. Whatever your party, however, it is often a good idea to invite the neighbours. This way you avoid any problem with complaints about the noise.

3. Select your menu.

Well in advance, and before sending out your invitations, decide upon your catering arrangements. If you are going to provide a lavish home-cooked supper, do warn your guests so that they don't dine beforehand. Likewise, don't let them starve in anticipation of a meal and then provide a few crisps and a cheese dip. A buffet is usually the best bet, with a varied cold collation of meats, savoury pies and flans, dips and dunks, various salads, cheeses, pâté and French bread, cold desserts, cheesecakes and a fresh fruit salad. This way you cater for every taste and appetite, and guests can help themselves as and when they feel like it.

4. Think of drink.

Any party needs liquid refreshment, although not necessarily of the alcoholic variety. A fruit punch always goes down well, and you can make a non-alcoholic one for drivers and guests who don't drink anything intoxicating. Here are a couple you might like to try:

Christmas Cup

    1 bottle of white wine
    1 large carton of fresh fruit juice – orange, grapefuit or pineapple depending upon your taste
    12 oz of sugar
    1 pint of tea
    4 tablespoons of brandy
    1 tablespoon of Angostura bitters
    Slices of orange and lemon

Mix all the ingredients together, pouring in freshly brewed strained tea and the Angostura bitters just before serving. Place in a warmed punch bowl and float orange and lemon slices on the top.

Driver's Drink (non-alcoholic)

    1 bottle of ginger ale
    $1\frac{1}{2}$ pints of boiling water
    $\frac{1}{2}$ lb of loaf sugar
    $\frac{1}{2}$ teacup of lime juice

Dissolve the sugar in the boiling water and allow to cool. Add the rest of the ingredients. Float some sprigs of mint on the top.

For a cold winter's evening your guests are sure to appreciate some mulled wine. Warm some red wine gently in a large saucepan, but DO NOT ALLOW TO BOIL. Add some powdered cinnamon, nutmeg and a little sugar to taste. Serve warm.

5. Plan your entertainment

Before your guests arrive, plan the evening carefully. Nothing is more embarrassing than having a room full of silent people occasionally making polite conversation, so make sure that they are kept amused throughout. As your guests arrive, introduce them to people already present and try to join them to one group with whom they have something particular in common. If you have children, get them to help by carrying round plates of canapés and nibbles. This helps break the ice, and if you serve them with a drink as soon as they arrive, this will get them in the party mood.

Arrange for a few games to be played. You'll find a whole selection at the end of the book. Not only are they fun to play but they are an excellent way of getting everyone joining in together.
6. Keep a little surprise.
The best host or hostess will always keep something back for the end of the party. It might be a culinary delight. When guests are starting to get tired, bring your party to a memorable conclusion by providing Irish coffee and a piece of Christmas cake. Or try to find out something special about one of your guests, saying for example: 'Now, not many people know this, even I didn't until this evening, but tonight is Malcolm and Dorothy's thirtieth wedding anniversary – so let's give them a little toast!' Or end your party with a sing-song of favourite carols. This will draw your party to a warm and logical conclusion, leaving people with happy memories of an enjoyable evening, rather than just fizzling out as guests drift away one by one.

The Day After the Night Before!

Whether it's a little excess port after Christmas dinner or too much champagne on New Year's Eve, there's nothing worse than waking up the following day with a mouth like a dustbin, a raw stomach and twenty men hammering inside your head! The best cure for a hangover is the advice given by William F. Buckley: 'Don't drink the night before'! But if the season of merrymaking is made just that little bit too merry – don't worry, there are some 'infallible cures' that can see you through the twelve days of Christmas.

The Hair of the Dog
Yes, there really is a 'hair of the dog' cure, although it is not from the dog that bit you. This is what you take:
    $1\frac{1}{2}$ fluid oz of whisky
    1 tablespoon of honey
    1 tablespoon of double cream
Blend together and drink.

Prairie Oyster
> 1 egg
> 1 tablespoon of Worcester sauce
> 1½ fluid oz port
> black pepper

Carefully slip the egg yolk into a wine glass without breaking it. Sprinkle a little black pepper. Add the Worcester sauce and the port. Knock back in one go without breaking the yolk. The whole experience makes you forget your hangover!

Rise and Shine
> 4 oz fresh orange juice
> 2 egg yolks

Mix together and drink in one foul swoop!

Avoiding a hangover should come under your Christmas planning, and by the time Christmas arrives, you've had a whole twelve months to discover what your limit is. As Dorothy Parker said: 'One more drink and I'd have been under the host!' Avoid that one too many!

Emergency Planning

Domestic disasters always happen to other people – or do they? On Christmas Day 1983 the O'Halloran family of Cleveland, Ohio, had just sat down to their Christmas dinner when the ceiling caved in, showering the family with plaster and completely destroying their feast. From Labrador dogs devouring the turkey to outbreaks of measles on Christmas Eve, true-life stories prove that this is not always the season of peace.

So, although it is unwise to anticipate doom and disaster, it can be as well to take a few precautions. Bearing in mind that shops are often closed for a considerable period over Christmas (though there is always a chemist's shop open somewhere, even if only for a couple of hours a day), make sure you have supplies of aspirin, sticking plaster, your favourite medicine for tummy upsets, and so on. Keep a list of emergency service numbers, from your doctor to the gas board and a plumber. Guard against any possibility of fire by checking the wiring of Christmas lights that have been packed away for a year – and unplug them before going to bed; put a fire guard round an open fire left unattended, and be especially careful with candles.

Stains

One accident almost bound to happen is that of things getting knocked over and spilt. Here's how to deal with some of the most common stains.

Ballpoint pen – Rub in a circular motion with methylated spirits.

Beer – Sponge with warm water.

Blood – On clothes, soak in a solution of cold salt water over night before washing normally. On carpets and furniture, sponge with cold water and then sprinkle flour on the stain. When dry, brush with a stiff brush.

Butter – Absorb the butter with fuller's earth and then wash in a biological detergent.

Candle grease – Scrape off with a blunt knife. If the grease has dripped onto a tablecloth, place a piece of blotting paper above and below the stain and run a warm iron over the top. This will absorb the grease.

Chocolate – Sponge with neat detergent, followed by cold water once the chocolate is removed. If the material is suitable, allow the chocolate to dry and then use a stiff brush to remove it. On clothes use a spray-on dry-cleaning powder.

Cream – Sponge with warm water and wash in a biological detergent.

Fruit juice – Sponge thoroughly with cold water. Do not use soap.

Gravy – Warm soapy solution. Try carbon tetrachloride if the stain is severe.

Ice Cream – Again, use carbon tetrachloride.

Jam – Use a borax solution.

Tomato sauce – Rub glycerine into the stain and leave overnight. Sponge off with detergent.

Urine – A new puppy for Christmas is sure to leave little puddles on the floor. Sponge with a solution of vinegar and water. Soda water will destroy any odours if rubbed on afterwards.

Wine – Sprinkle salt or French chalk on the stain whilst still wet, brush off when dry. Sponge with warm soap solution first.

DECK THE HALLS
WITH
BOUGHS OF HOLLY

CHRISTMAS CARDS

The first sign each year that Christmas is fast approaching is the sight of the postman staggering up your path with a bulging sack of cards. Unless you are extremely popular, it is unlikely that they will be all for you, but there is no more warming sound than the plip-plop of cards dropping onto the mat, and the familiar sight of the handwriting of old friends.

Writing to friends at Christmas and sending a seasonal message of good wishes has a long history. In pagan times during the winter solstice it was customary to exchange small charms or good-luck tokens. In the tombs of the Pharaohs symbolic Christmas gifts have been discovered bearing the inscription '*Au ab nab*', which means 'All good luck'. These charms were meant to bring good luck during the coming New Year.

New Year cards were first produced from fine engravings in the fifteenth century, and although bearing the inscription 'A good and happy New Year', they also bore a picture of the infant Jesus in his crib and clearly alluded to the birth of Christ. Many of these beautiful hand-painted cards have survived because they were kept in Bibles as bookmarks. The practice of giving New Year cards continued through to the seventeenth century, but it was in the eighteenth century that we find the first card produced on a commercial basis, and it was not long before a whole host of groups decided to cash in on this new idea. Soon tradesmen, from lamp-lighters to firemen, were leaving their greeting card at houses in the hope of getting a Christmas 'box' or tip.

On the domestic scene, people corresponding with friends and relatives began to use decorated notepaper with a Christmas theme, but the vast amount of letter-writing required soon became too laborious for the early Victorians, and so with the expansion of the Post Office in the 1840s, the Christmas card as we know it came into being. With a printed greeting, all it needed was a signature.

The first Christmas card appeared in 1843 and was the brainchild of one Henry Cole, an eccentric Victorian who also came up with the idea of perforated postage stamps and postcards. Cole conceived the idea and got an artist called John Calcott

Horsley to execute it. It was printed in lithography by Jobbins of Warwick Court, Holborn, and handcoloured by a professional 'colourer' called Mason. The edition was 'published at Felix Summerley's Home Treasury Office, 12 Old Bond Street, London' by a friend of Henry Cole's named Joseph Cundall, who claimed that 'many copies were sold, but possibly not more than 1,000'. It bore the simple inscription 'A Merry Christmas and a Happy New Year to You' and cost one shilling (5p), which was actually a lot of money 150 years ago.

The craze for sending Christmas cards took off, and soon cards were actually being reviewed in the national press! The newest Christmas tradition is now one of the most popular, and millions of cards are now sent each year, bearing every conceivable kind of illustration from Dickensian snow scenes to less conventional cartoons of drunken choirboys and obese Father Christmases stuck in chimneys.

One of the most popular designs on any card is that of the little Robin Redbreast, who first made his appearance on a card in 1862. Legend says that a robin tried to ease Christ's pain on the way to the Crucifixion by pulling a thorn from His crown of thorns. A drop of the Saviour's blood fell onto the robin's breast, and it has remained red ever since. Delightful though the story is, it does not explain the connection with Christ's birth. It probably stems from the fact that a robin's feather was often thought to bring good luck (rather like a rabbit's foot today), and ancient rhymes show how sacred the robin was:

The robin aye the redbreast,
The robin and the wren,
If ye take out the nest,
Ye'll never thrive again.

The earliest rhymes in Christmas cards were actually about robins too. This appeared in the 1860s:

My wishes come by Robin's rhymes,
Since he was pleased so many times;
For London poor are still in need,
Whom Robin's crumbs may help to feed.

41

Or if the missions we would aid,
By Christmas cards and sheets now made,
The Robin gladly will take flight,
With wings of love he'll bear your mite.

Each Christmas offering to our King,
Each feeble prayer may blessings bring;
May blessings rest on you, my friend,
True Christmas joys that never end.

It wasn't long before the sentiment inside the card became far more important than the picture on the outside, and recipients of the cards read the verse inside very carefully. Although Tennyson was once offered 1,000 guineas for a couple of Christmas card verses, most of the writers remained anonymous amateurs. The most prolific writer was a shy, deaf lady called Helen Marion Burnside, who became the Queen of Cards and is known to have penned over six thousand verses between 1874 and 1900.

Here are some classic Christmas card greetings from those early days:

It's an old, old wish
On a tiny little card.
It's simply 'Merry Christmas',
But I wish it awfully hard.

*　*　*

We have waited
　For thy coming,
Though brief must be
　Thy reign,
Father Christmas,
　Bright and cheery,
Welcome! Welcome!
　Once again!

Merry Christmas!
　Happy Christmas!
Blessed, holy,

Christmas-tide!
When the spirit
  Of the season,
Sitteth by
  Each fireside!

(A.H. Baldwin, 1880)

* * *

Oh, yes, well do I remember
  Your joyful voice and heartfelt glee;
Accept, then, in this bleak December,
  A merry Christmas, dear, from me.

* * *

Some guide the brush and some the pen,
  Some sing in chorus high;
I beg a plume from every wing,
  But cannot learn to fly;
Yet well I know my Christmas wish
  Is just as fond and true
As Art or Pen could e'er express,
  Because inspired by you!

* * *

Oh, Life is but a river;
And in our childhood, we
But a fair running streamlet
Adorn'd with flowers see.

But as we grow more earnest,
The river grows more deep;
And where we laugh'd in childhood,
We, older, pause to weep.

Each Christmas as it passes,
Some change to us doth bring;
Yet to our friends the closer,
As Time creeps on, we cling.

*   *   *

A happy Christmas to my friend,
And countless blessings, without end.

*   *   *

We seem too busy every day
To say the things we want to say;
Our deepest thoughts we seem to hide
Until we reach the Christmas-tide.
'Tis then we send to friends again
In happy words the Old Refrain –
'A Very Merry Christmas'

*   *   *

Christmas comes! While you are sleeping,
In the holy Angel's keeping,
He around your bed is creeping,
And within the curtains peeping,
Leaving for all good girls and boys
Such merry games and pretty toys.

Although composed in the last century, many of the Victorian verses contain warm sentiments that we still want to express today.

Not all Victorian cards were moral or sentimental. One from the end of the nineteenth century depicted a somewhat obese, bewhiskered stockbroker, dressed as an angel, dancing and singing:

I hope you will not think it strange,
If I fly from the Stock Exchange,
To bring you the news surprising,
That all the New Year bonds are rising!

Comic cards became very popular, and the Victorians were masters at inventing trick and mechanical cards which were ingenious in their construction and often very elaborate, rather like children's pop-up books from which whole three-dimensional scenes appear. Some concealed bouquets of flowers that revealed themselves in life-like colour when the card was open; one even portrayed a little boy who literally appears to climb out of the card as you hold it. Queen Mary had a vast collect of beautiful and unusual cards, many of which were mechanical, that are now in the British Museum.

Making Cards

A popular Victorian pastime was, of course, making Christmas cards, and a hundred years later more and more people are starting to make their own cards again. With a little care your original cards can look crisp and professional. The secret of home-made cards is to make them look delicate and attractive. Large, thick cards look cheap and crude, and create totally the wrong impression.

Here are the golden rules of making your own cards:

Always use proper thin card on which to work. Don't try to make do with any old card that you happen to have by you – it will look like the rubbish it is. Visit an art shop and buy a few sheets of thin card.

Keep your cards small. A tiny, beautifully made card is very impressive and will be appreciated by the recipient. If you look in the shops, small cards are often the most expensive!

Use very sharp scissors or a razor blade for precise cuts. Never use old blunt scissors. Your work will look shoddy.

If using glue, use the kind that will not cause your card to bend or buckle when it dries.

Don't try to make your cards too elaborate.

Measure accurately. Nothing looks worse that a warped or lopsided card!

The Verse

The most difficult part of the card is often putting the verse inside, because if you're not careful, this can really show your card up to look amateurish. NEVER paste the verse from an old Christmas card inside, and don't type the verse.

If you, or a member of your family, have beautiful handwriting, use a mapping pen and write out your verse in stylish writing. If not, keep your message very simple and use a stencil or letraset. You can buy sheets of letters which can make your cards look very professional indeed. Alternatively you can have a rubber stamp made with your greeting on. This will involve a couple of pounds initial expense, but once you've got it, you can go on producing Christmas cards for life.

One important tip is to put your message or verse inside the card *before* you start work on the outside. Nothing is worse than spending hours creating a gorgeous design on the front, and then end up making a blotch with the ink as you write the greeting!

Silhouette Card

To create a simple, yet attractive card, all you need is an aerosol can of gold or silver paint. Lay your blank card face up on a sheet of paper and prepare to spray a silhouette onto it.

To do this you can lay a pretty cake doily over the card. Spray lightly with the paint, and when you remove the doily, the design will be left on the card. For something a little more imaginative, cut out the shape of a leaf or a star from the doily and use this as a stencil.

Another simple but effective design requires a few real leaves, such as holly and ivy. Take a piece of green card and lay out the leaves in a pattern on the card. Spray the whole card and the leaves with gold paint and leave to dry. When you remove the leaves, you will be left with a gold card and the silhouettes of the leaves in green. The same leaves can be used over and over again in different designs to make a whole number of cards. When you've finished making the cards, the gold leaves can be used as Christmas decorations.

Finally, using the stencil idea, you can make yourself a stencil of the words 'HAPPY CHRISTMAS' by cutting them out of a piece of card and spraying through with your aerosol.

Cut-Out Card

Take your piece of card and fold it in half from top to bottom, so that when you stand the card up, the fold will be at the top rather than at the side. Draw or paint onto your card a Christmas figure, such as an angel, a Santa Claus, a snowman, even a Christmas tree, and cut out the shape, making sure that you leave at least part of the fold at the top to prevent the card falling apart. Decorate the card as attractively as you can.

Front   Side view

Candle Card
There is something magical about making candle cards that children enjoy. Use white card for your base and draw your design onto the card with a white wax candle. Paint the card with a thin-coat of a coloured water-based paint, and your wax design will magically appear.

Tissue Paper Cards
Using different coloured pieces of tissue paper, cut out some Christmas shapes, stars, baubles, holly etc., and using only very small amounts of glue, stick them onto your card. If you allow the different coloured tissues to overlap, some very interesting designs can be produced. If you are intending to make a lot of cards, put several sheets of tissue paper together, draw the design you intend to cut out on the top piece, and then cut out the shape through all the layers. This way you can mass-produce stars and shapes without having to cut out each individually.

Holly Cards
Take some holly leaves and press them flat, either by placing them in a flower-press or by simply placing them underneath a pile of heavy books for several days. When they are ready, coat them with a clear varnish to preserve them, and then stick them down onto your card. Two or three per card are quite sufficient. Add a few dots of red nail-varnish to represent the berries, and stick a red ribbon bow in the top left-hand corner for a very expensive-looking card.

Mosaic Cards
Another card that children will really enjoy making. All you need are hundreds of tiny scraps of torn paper, cut from tissue or crêpe paper of different colours. Draw the outline of your design onto the card in pencil, and then fill in the outline with your little pieces of paper to form a mosaic. Try to use the correct colour paper. For example, if you are going to do a robin, use red paper for the breast, but don't simply use one shade of red: instead use three or four different shades. The mixture of different reds will look very

striking. Another tip for sticking down the mosaics is not to put the paste on each individual scrap of paper as you stick it down, but spread a thin coat over the card first and then stick the scraps to that. A glue-stick rubbed over the design first will be far less messy than using glue. Do allow the card to dry thoroughly for a couple of days before placing in an envelope and posting.

Blackmail Card

No, you are not going to blackmail someone for money over Christmas! Take some newspapers and magazines and cut out different letters to form a greeting for your card. Paste the letters onto the front and cover the whole card with a coating of clear varnish. An excellent card to send to someone who is a journalist!

Christmas Cracker Card

Take a long strip of card and fold the sides towards the middle:

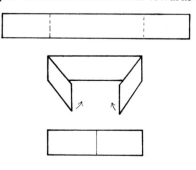

With the card in the position that it will be when closed, carefully cut it into the shape of a Christmas cracker:

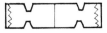

Decorate it with paints or coloured paper to look like a cracker and write the word

inside so that it looks like a cracker when opened!

Wool Cards

Draw your design or greeting on the front of your card and, using lengths of wool or string, press them down firmly with glue onto the card to produce a raised design. You can make your design in wool and then paint or spray the whole card, or use different coloured wools to fill in the design. A Father Christmas created out of just red and white wool would look very effective indeed. If you are feeling very adventurous, a large card cut into the shape of a tree can be covered with tufts of green wool, and then coloured wool pompoms can be made to decorate it. Wool cards do not, however, travel well through the post so it is a good idea to only give them to people by hand.

Father Christmas Card

First take your basic card and paint it black, and stick on a few silver stars to form a night sky. From a separate piece of card, cut out the shape of a slanting roof with a large chimney:

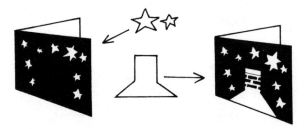

Stick this onto the card, but do not glue the top of the chimney down, so that it forms a little pocket:

Glue edges only,
leaving top open

Next cut out a little cardboard Father Christmas carrying a sack, and write a personalized Christmas greeting on his sack. Finally, tuck him into the chimney before sending the card.

Snowman Card

To make a very long and effective card, take a piece of card as long as you can find and fold it into a concertina effect:

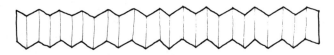

On the top of the card draw the outline of a snowman or a tree, even good old Santa Claus, and cut through all the layers:

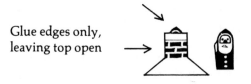

When you open out the card, you will have a row of snowmen which you can decorate as you please:

CHRISTMAS DECORATIONS

The Christmas Tree

The evergreen tree has long been a symbol of everlasting life, and in most homes the Christmas tree is one of the most popular of all decorations. Legend says that in the eighth century St Boniface, on a mission to Germany, came across a group of pagans worshipping an oak tree and about to sacrifice the life of a small child. Heroically, St Boniface, like an eighth-century Superman, leapt to the child's rescue, grabbed the sacrificial axe and chopped down the oak tree. The life of the child was saved, and on stooping to pick him up, St Boniface noticed, growing between the roots of the severed oak, a tiny spruce tree. As a symbol of new life, it soon became linked with Christmas and has now become an indispensable part of Christmas.

As with many traditions, it was not until the nineteenth century that the tree became a feature of the decorations in the British Isles. Decorated trees were popular in Germany for centuries, and in 1605 a German merchant recorded in his diary, 'At Christmas they set up fir trees in Strasbourg and hang on them roses cut out of many-coloured paper, apples, wafers, gold-foil and sweets.' It was Prince Albert who brought the idea from his native Germany to Britain, and the notion of having a Christmas tree soon caught on. The Royal family are still keen supporters of the Christmas tree, and to this day the Queen gives two trees to the Dean of St Paul's Cathedral for him to display and for her subjects to enjoy. If truth be told, many of her subjects who see the St Paul's trees probably don't appreciate that they are a royal gift, although there can be few who haven't heard about that other celebrated London Christmas tree that has been donated annually by the people of Oslo since 1946 and stands proudly in Trafalgar Square until Twelfth Night.

One of the nicest traditions concerning Christmas trees is that of allowing children to decorate them. In the last century, when trees were lit with real candles, children did not see the tree until it was lit and fully decorated, but today it is a magical moment to watch a child's eyes sparkle like baubles as they help with the decorations, not only in putting them on but with making them too.

Tree Decorations

Baubles

Take ping-pong balls (they don't have to be new) and make a small hole in the top of each of them. Open up some small paper-clips so that they make a figure-of-eight shape, and push one half of the clip through the hole and into the ball:

Now dip the ball into gold paint, or spray it if you prefer, and before the paint is dry, sprinkle on some gold glitter. When completely dry, hang on your tree.

Snowflakes

Cut out a circle from a paper cake doily and fold up like a concertina:

Pull the two ends round and glue them together:

Make two of these and glue them together. Thread a piece of cotton through and hang them on the tree.

Paper Garland

Make a long strip of crêpe paper by cutting off lengths and gluing them together. Fold the strip into a concertina and cut a pattern around the edge:

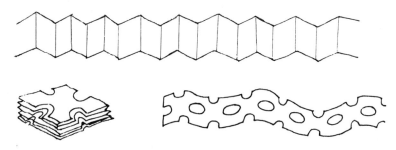

Unfold it and twist the garland as you drape it around the tree.

Silver Bells

During the period before Christmas, keep any old cream cartons and yoghurt pots that you may have. Wash them out carefully and, when completely dry, spray them with silver paint. Dip the rim in silver glitter. Hang upside down with thread, and you have a silver bell.

Miniature Crackers

Make small tubes of cardboard and secure them with sellotape. Roll up in brightly coloured paper and secure the ends with cotton. If you wish, the crackers can be filled with small sweets and chocolates.

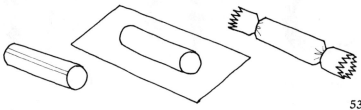

Spider's Web

Skill and patience will be rewarded with this beautiful decoration. Begin by gluing three cocktail sticks into a star shape and allow to dry completely. Take a piece of strong thread and tie it to the centre of the star. Wind it a couple of centimetres up the first stick, wind it round twice, then move across to the next stick and wind it twice around that, and so on until you have completed one circle. Move the thread up another centimetre and make another circle in the same way, until gradually you have built up a web:

Leave one long end of thread at the end to hang it from the tree. Spray the whole web with silver paint and dip in glitter to give it that added lustre of a real web. You can use longer sticks to make a bigger web to suspend from the corner of a room as an added and co-ordinated decoration, and if you really want to enchant the children, you can paint four pipe-cleaners black and twist them together to make an eight-legged spider!

Silver Rings

From an old toilet roll, or the empty tube from a used kitchen roll, cut out a number of rings so that they look rather like serviette rings. Cover each of the rings with silver foil and then push two together at right-angles to each other.

Tie a ribbon around the top and suspend it from the tree.

Christmas Angel

Some people put a silver star on the top of their tree to represent the star that guided the Three Wise Men to Bethlehem. (This can be made easily by cutting out a star from cardboard and covering it with silver foil. Crinkle the foil so that it reflects the light.) But tradition says that spruce trees have woodland spirits to keep them alive. As spirits have wings, and so do angels, the Christmas angel should really adorn the top of your tree. Any small doll can be dressed to make an angel. To make the bodice of the dress, simply take a strip of material and cross it over the chest. For the skirt, cut out a large circle of material by drawing round a plate. Cut a hole in the centre and slip it over the doll. An elastic band around the waist should secure it and can be used to fasten her to the topmost branch of the tree. Cut out some cardboard wings, cover them in tinfoil and glue them to her back, and a strip of tinsel as a halo around her head will complete your angel.

Household Decorations

Holly

Holly (*Ilex aquifolium*) is more than just a Christmas decoration for it is said to have healing properties. Its presence in your house is said to ward off asthma, dropsy, gout, rheumatism and the measles, and a sprig of it on your front door will protect your home from thunder, lightning, fire and the 'evil eye'. If you are single and want to know whom you will marry, never fear, for holly has the power to solve that problem too. All you have to do is pick nine holly leaves at midnight on a Friday night, tie them in nine knots in a three-cornered handkerchief and put the whole lot under your pillow. That night a vision of your future partner will appear in your dreams. Don't spoil your Christmas: if you don't like the look of him or her, you can break the spell by telling someone about it *before* breakfast next morning!

Ivy

Ivy (*Hedera helix*) also has healing properties. If you bind corns with ivy leaves, they will go away, and a wreath of ivy in your hair will prevent baldness. You might get greenfly and some funny looks, but you'll never go bald! Ivy will also lead a girl to her future husband. At any time between the Feast of St Nicholas (6 December) and Twelfth Night (6 January) a girl can hold a piece of ivy to her heart and say:

Ivy, Ivy, I love you.
In my bosom I put you.
The first young man who speaks to me,
My future husband he shall be.

And if she's got any sense, she'll dash straight to the young man she would most like to marry, otherwise she could end up with the milkman!

Mistletoe
(*Viscum album*) A popular novelty at any office Christmas party, mistletoe not only provides an opportunity to kiss anyone you fancy but will also protect you from witches and black magic, ward off epilepsy and St Vitus' Dance (not another Christmas ball!) and promote peace and harmony.

Yule Log
With the advent of central heating, the burning of Yule logs has vanished from our Christmas customs. As we saw in Chapter 1, in the days of real log fires a special Yule log was chosen and was burnt ceremoniously on Christmas Eve. It brought good luck for the future and signified the end of old feuds and the start of new friendships. So that the Yule log tradition doesn't die, traditionalists like to have a symbolic log in their homes at Christmas. Many have a cake in the form of a chocolate log, but the nearest to a real Yule log is to take a genuine piece of wood about one foot long and four inches high (a small log is perfect, of course), bore two or three small holes in the top and push in some red candles. Decorate the log with artificial snow (a little white paint, or a few dabs of wet plaster of Paris), some real holly and ivy, a couple of Christmas tree baubles and red ribbon bow. The candles can be lit on Christmas Eve, and the old Yule tradition will not have died.

Artificial Trees
It is not always practicable to have a real Christmas tree, and the kind of artificial ones that can be bought may be either too expensive or simply too big for a small flat or house. If with the traumas of Christmas preparations you don't feel up to buying and decorating a real tree, coping with fused fairy-lights and dropped pine-needles, with a little time and very little effort you can create

your own tree.

The simplest of all is to create a space-saving wall-hanging tree. From a large piece of card, cut out the shape of a tree and paint it green or cover it with green crêpe paper. You can then stick, pin or staple festoons and decorations onto it. Let your imagination run riot! When it is finished, simply hang it on the wall with a drawing-pin or a piece of Blu-tack.

To create a three-dimensional tree, make a cone out of a piece of cardboard. First, cut out a large circle of card. From one edge to the centre make a single cut in a straight line. Overlap the card at this slit until you have a cone. Staple it in place.

Cut up some squares of green tissue paper, each approximately one inch square. Screw each square into a little ball, and stick them all over your cone. Start at the bottom edge and work upwards towards the point until the cone is completely covered. When it is dry, you can decorate it with baubles and tinsel which can be pinned on with ordinary pins or, if it is for children, sellotaped or glued on. When it is decorated, you can stand the tree over a small flower-pot decorated with red crêpe paper.

A similar but less time-consuming tree can be made by using a cardboard cone as a base as before and covering it with crêpe paper. Take strips of crêpe paper and fold them in half lengthways and snip it all the way along like this:

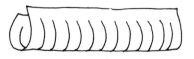

Glue the top edge of the strips together and then glue them around the tree, again starting at the base and working your way up to the point. Stand over a pot and decorate as before.

The same idea can be used to make a two-dimensional tree by cutting out the shape of a tree from a large sheet of card and sticking the strips across it.

Paper Chains

An old favourite, paper chains are as popular as they ever were and fun to make for both young and old alike. Paper chains are useful for festooning trees, brightening walls, framing windows and doors and draping across the ceilings. Packets of gummed paper in bright colours can be bought from stationers especially for making paper chains, but you can use strips of wrapping paper or crêpe paper, or even strips from coloured paper bags. Make the first loop by gluing the two ends of a strip together. Thread the next strip of paper through the loop and join its ends together. Gradually you can build up a chain as long or as short as you like.

For something slightly more ambitious you can try weaving paper chains using two different colours of crêpe paper, red and green, or red and white, for example. You will need two strips of crêpe paper, one of each colour, about an inch wide and each as long as possible. Begin by placing the two ends at right angles to each other and glue them together:

Now fold the bottom strip up over the top strip, then the left strip over the right, then the top over the bottom, then the right over the left, then the bottom over the top, and so on until you reach the end, when you can glue the ends of the strips of paper together and unfurl your glorious chain.

Paper Baubles
Draw around the rim of a glass onto a sheet of coloured tissue paper and cut out the circles. Cut each circle in half, and from each half make a cone by gluing two edges together. Thread one cone onto a length of thread at the point, and continue joining the cones together until a large ball is formed. Leave a loop of thread so that the ball can be hung up.

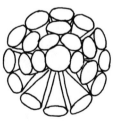

Christmas Card Pennants

Knowing where to put Christmas cards is always a problem. If stood around a room, they look crowded and often buckle with the heat. You can make a pennant from a long strip of coloured paper or fabric about six inches across and three to four feet long. Put a bow at the top and cut it into the shape of a ribbon at the bottom. Cards can be pinned on or attached with Blu-tack as they arrive:

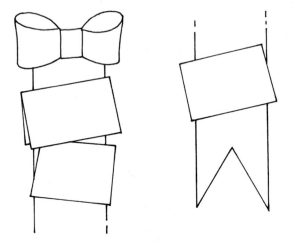

Alternatively, and much simpler, a length of red ribbon can be attached with a couple of drawing-pins from the ceiling to the floor, to which your cards can be attached with paper-clips.

Paper Stars

Stars always look Christmassy, and they look very attractive hanging from windows, lampshades and trees. Making a star is very simple. Take a cake doily and fold it into eight, then cut out a triangle, like this:

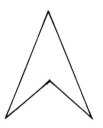

When you open it up, you will have an eight-pointed star which can be sprayed or painted as you wish.

Paper Wreaths

Begin by cutting out three strips of variously coloured paper about two feet long and two inches wide. Wrap some sellotape around one end of the three strips to bind them together and then plait them. Sellotape the other end and join the two pieces together to form a circle. Tie a large ribbon to cover the joins and suspend a silver star or a bauble in the centre to make it look festive. Use Blu-tack to fix the wreath to your door. If you are feeling very ambitious, you can weave sprigs of holly and ivy into your wreath.

Christmas Crib

Making a crib can provide hours of fun for children, and of course helps them with their understanding of the Nativity and the true meaning of Christmas. Cribs can be as simple or as elaborate as time and materials will allow. The simplest base for a crib can be a shoebox painted to look like a stable, with a window and night sky at the back. Real straw or shredded paper can be placed on the floor. The figures and animals can be made from pipe-cleaners, plasticine or modelling clay, or can be cut out from card:

The manger can be made from the drawer of a matchbox and four used matchsticks.

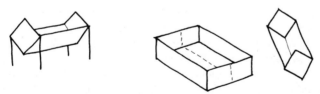

If you have more than one child, more than one scene can be created: one the shepherds on the hillside, the next the stable as above, and finally the Three Kings in a desert setting with palm trees, following the star to Bethlehem. In many European homes the Christmas crib is the most important decoration of all.

Advent Calendar
From 1 December until Christmas Eve children can count off the days to Christmas by using an Advent calendar. These are simple to make and provide twenty-four days of fun and anticipation.

To make an Advent calendar, take two pieces of thin card and on the first one draw a house with twenty-three small windows and one large door. Number each window 1 to 23 (not necessarily in consecutive order) and the door 24. Cut around three sides of each window so that it makes a little flap that can be opened. To make it easier a metal paper-fastener can be put through each window so that it looks like a little brass knob:

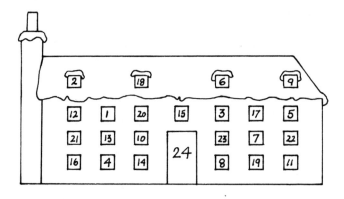

On the second sheet of card will be the contents of each window. Place the first sheet over the second and with a pencil trace round the outline of the windows and the door. On the base card you will then need to draw twenty-four little pictures showing the preparations up to Christmas, or stick on scenes from old Christmas cards so that there is a different scene for each day. Whatever you do, the scene for 24 December must be the Nativity scene. When you have finished each scene, stick the first card onto the second, taking care to line up the windows. Close all the doors and then let the children open them one a day until Christmas.

Table Decorations

Place mats

For your festive table the centre of each person's setting is dominated by their place mat, so it is a nice idea to discard your usual mats and replace them with something more seasonal. Old floor tiles or pieces of hardboard make ideal bases, and on this occasion it does not really matter if your mats are not all identical in size. From last year's Christmas cards, pick out the largest, or cut pieces from them to make a collage, and stick the Christmas picture you have chosen down onto your base. Carefully smooth over the top a piece of clear sticky-back plastic, or give them several coats of clear varnish, and you have festive place mats that will last for years.

Cutlery Holder

Take a tube from an empty kitchen roll and cut out a hole in the top so that the cutlery can rest on it. Stick the roll to a flat piece of card and cover it all with foil or paint it:

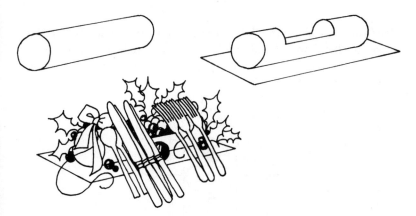

Fill the tube with sweets or little gifts, and decorate the cardboard base with holly, baubles and ribbons.

Napkin Holder
To make a Father Christmas napkin holder, take a piece of thin card and cut it to this shape:

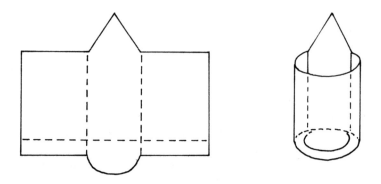

Fold the card along the dotted lines and fold the side pieces around the back and glue them together. Bend the back curved piece at the bottom and fix it in position by gluing it to the little tabs. Make the arms by cutting out two pieces of card to look like this:

Fold the arms along the dotted line and glue the folded bits to the sides of the body. Paint on his face and red suit, glue on a cottonwool beard and bobble on his hat, and Father Christmas is ready for the table.

If you don't use him for napkins, he can always be filled with sweets or after-dinner mints.

Christmas Drink Mat

Make sixteen small shapes like this out of stiff paper. Cover each with foil, eight gold and eight silver, and glue them one on top of the other to make a mat for your Christmas wine.

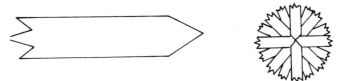

Christmas Crackers

No Christmas table would be complete without crackers. In 1840 a confectioner named Thomas Smith was on a business trip to Paris. Working with confectionery, he was very intrigued by a French delicacy, a sugared almond, known as a 'bonbon' which the French gave to each other as little love tokens. Thomas Smith brought some 'bonbons' over to England, and as a sales gimmick he gave a little love motto with each sweet. This charming idea soon caught on, and soon he came up with the idea of giving little toys and novelties with mottoes. This venture was not a success, and so he decided he would have to think up a new idea to make his toys sell.

It was one Christmas Day that the idea of a Christmas cracker was literally sparked off when a jet of resin from his log fire burst into flame with a loud 'crack!'. Using this idea, he decided to make a log-shaped package that would produce a surprise bang, and inside would be a 'bonbon' and a motto. After many experiments he finally succeeded in creating a safe cracker, and the Christmas cracker as we know it, complete with paper hat, was invented. It soon became a firm favourite at parties and by the end of the nineteenth century his cracker company, the only one of its kind in the world, was producing nearly fourteen million crackers a year and exporting them abroad. His factory in Norfolk is still producing crackers and now employs over a thousand people.

Crackers now come in all shapes and sizes. Smith once produced one that was thirty feet high and had a spiral staircase inside and was eventually 'cracked' by a series of pulleys that detonated an explosion. Inside were very expensive toys, and by all accounts it was an incredible spectacle. In 1974, however, Smith was outcracked when a cracker forty-five feet long was built for the BBC children's programme 'Record Breakers'. A forty-two-foot long cracker was built in 1972 that actually contained a Ford Escort car!

To make your own crackers, all you need are some cardboard tubes and crêpe paper. Fill the rolls with sweets, cover them with the crêpe paper and secure the ends. Decorate the crackers with silver paper and ribbon. The most important part of a cracker is, of course, the 'crack'. Unfortunately for cracker-lovers, but fortunately for safety standards, it is illegal to sell anything that contains gunpowder, and so it is impossible to buy the real thing. You can always buy some very cheap crackers and remove the 'cracks' very carefully, but it is just as much fun to all shout 'BANG!' very loudly as you pull your crackers.

One final ingredient which no cracker should be without is the Christmas motto. Here are some corny cracks that are sure to make your crackers go with a bang:

Why is it dangerous for a car to stop?
Because it brakes (breaks).

What was the name of the famous Jewish detective?
Shylock Holmes.

Why is an envelope like a snooty person?
When it is stuck up.

What is the best way to remove paint?
Sit down on it before it is dry.

Why can't ducks fly upside down?
Because they would quack up.

What did the one-eared man say when he was offered a drink?
'No thanks, I've got one 'ere.'

Why did the cleaner stop cleaning?
Because she found that grime doesn't pay.

How do you hire a horse?
Put four bricks under it.

What is brown and sounds like a bell?
Dung.

How do you join the Navy?
Handcuff the sailors together.

What has four legs and flies?
A dead horse and two pairs of trousers.

What is the fastest string in the world?
Con-cord.

If a girl falls down a well, why can't her brother help her out?
Because he can't be a brother and assist her too.

What did the man say when he staggered into the Queen's Arms?
'Very kind of you, Your Majesty.'

What do you call a Scottish cloakroom-attendant?
Angus MaCoatup.

What's green and goes hith?
A snake with a lisp.

How does a flea get from one place to another?
By itch-hiking.

Whatever the year, whatever the class, Christmas dinner has always been a meal to look forward to and remember. During the Victorian era, many of the most humble families could sit down to roast goose on Christmas Day, thanks to one of those venerable working-class institutions known as the 'Goose Club', into which workers paid a little each week and then received a goose, sometimes even a bottle of port, at Christmas, which they would not otherwise have been able to afford. Although the 'Goose Club' has long since gone out of fashion, many shops and communities still run a Christmas club that ensures that anyone who finds saving money difficult will be assured of a good feast on 25 December.

Wining and dining are for us as much a part of Christmas as holly, cards and presents; it is said that more time is spent preparing Christmas dinner than any other meal throughout the year. An Italian adage, always quoted when anyone has a lot to do (we say we have 'a lot on our plate') is: 'She's as busy as an English oven at Christmas', and looking back through the ages, English ovens have certainly been busy. At Windsor Castle on Christmas Day, Queen Victoria and her family would sit down to soup, sole or haddock, followed by roast swan or roast beef, then a choice of pheasant, partridge, capon, rabbit, veal or chicken, with side dishes of brawn, mutton, sausages and pork. Having waded through this lot, they would still find room for savoury pies and a dessert! Every year, too, a traditional centrepiece of the Christmas dinner would be the boar's head, which in 1898 was actually shot on the Queen's own land at Windsor.

By our standards Queen Victoria may have had a large table, but a former monarch of England, King John, in 1206 is said to have had on his table one hundred pigs, one hundred sheep, one thousand chickens and twenty oxen! This was simply to feed the King and his court in Winchester Castle!

The turkey that we associate with our Christmas dinners is quite a recent innovation as far as Christmas traditions go. The turkey was introduced from Spain (having originally come from South America) during the early part of the sixteenth century, and was first eaten in England in around 1535. It was not until the mid-nineteenth century that the turkey we all know and love became a popular festive dish. It was around this time that the pattern for our own Christmas catering became established. One person who really knew how to do things in style, and whose traditions we still follow, was one Mary Isabella Beeton, the ever popular 'Mrs Beeton'.

The name 'Mrs Beeton' automatically conjures up the vision of a plump, rosy-cheeked old woman, yet few people realize that the great Victorian gourmet died in 1864 aged only twenty-eight. This remarkable woman was not only a great domestic scientist, she was also a noted pianist and a very successful journalist. Had she, but lived, who knows what heights Mrs B would have reached? Her masterpiece was, of course, the classic *Book of Household Management*, in which she not only reveals the secrets of successful catering but pours out invaluable advice to any would-be host or hostess:

'Hospitality is a most excellent virtue, but care must be taken that the love of company, for its own sake, does not become a prevailing passion; for then the habit is no longer hospitality, but dissipation.

'In conversation, trifling occurrences, such as small disappointments, petty annoyances, and other everyday incidents, should never be mentioned to friends. Greater events, whether of joy or sorrow, should be communicated to friends; and, on such occasions, their sympathy gratifies and comforts. If the mistress be a wife never let a word in connection with her husband's failures pass her lips; and in cultivating the powers of conversation, she should keep the versified counsel of Cowper continually in her memory – that it:

Should flow like water after summer showers,
Not as if raised by mere mechanic powers.'

Good, sound advice even today! As a cook, her rules for the kitchen still ring true too:
1. Without cleanliness and punctuality good cooking is impossible.
2. Leave nothing dirty; clean and clear as you go.
3. A time for everything, and everything in time.
4. A good cook wastes nothing.
5. An hour lost in the morning has to be run after all day.
6. Haste without hurry saves worry, fuss and flurry.
7. Stew boiled is stew spoiled.

8. Strong fire for roasting; clear fire for broiling.

Although few have the facilities or the resources to prepare the kind of Christmas dinners that Mrs Beeton used to serve, it's a mouth-watering experience to look at the delicious menus that she used to come up with. The menus are given in English and French:

Christmas Dinners for Eight:

I.

Mock-turtle soup	*Potage de Tête de Veau*
Turbot	*Turbot*
Lobster Sauce	*Sauce Homard*
Vol-au-vent of Oysters	*Vol-au-vent aux Huîtres*
Salmi of Larks	*Salmis d'Alouettes*
Saddle of Mutton	*Selle de Mouton*
Pheasants	*Faisans*
Farced Olives	*Olives Farcies*
Curaçao Soufflé	*Soufflé au Curaçao*
Chocolate Cream	*Crême au Chocolat*
Diablotins	*Diablotins*

II

Caviare	*Caviare*
Purée of Wood Pigeons	*Purée de Ramier*
Boiled Filleted Soles	*Soles à la Crême*
Cream Sauce	*Eperlans*
Smelts	*Boudins à la Reine*
Minced Fowl	*Salmis de Coqs de Bruyère*
Hashed Grouse	*Bifteck*
Rump Steak	*Sauce aux Huîtres*
Oyster Sauce	*Perdraux*
Partridges	*Salade*
Salad	*Charlotte Russe*
Charlotte Russe	*Gelée au Citron*
Lemon Jelly	*Anges en Chevaux*
Angels on Horseback	

Christmas Dinners for Six:
III.

Caviare	*Caviare*
Lobster Soup	*Bisque de Homard*
Tench stewed with Wine	*Tanche au Vin Blanc*
Partridge Cream	*Crême de Perdraux*
Pâté de Foie Gras	*Pâté de Foie Gras*
Saddle of Mutton	*Selle de Mouton*
Snipe	*Bécassines*
Anchovy Salad	*Salade aux Anchois*
Cabinet Pudding	*Pouding Anglais*
Benedictine Iced Soufflé	*Soufflé Glacé à la Benedictine*
Diablotins	*Diablotins*

IV.

Oxtail Soup	*Soup de Tête de Boeuf*
Soles with Cream Sauce	*Soles à la Crême*
Stuffed Tomatoes	*Tomates Farcies*
Beef Olives	*Olives de Boeuf*
Loin of Mutton	*Longe de Mouton*
Teal	*Sarcelles*
Orange Fritters	*Beignets d'Oranges*
Plum Pudding	*Pouding à la Valentia*
Cheese Salad	*Salade au Fromage*

These impressive menus can easily be adapted and modified for a twentieth-century Christmas dinner party, by simply serving *some* instead of all of the courses. Mrs Beeton's recommendations for family menus over the festive season still have a very practical use, and would be ideal for the week following Christmas. Substitute 'Pheasant' with left-over turkey or chicken!

Sunday:	Mock-turtle soup
	Roast ribs of beef
	Brussels sprouts, potatoes
	Mince pies, jelly
Monday:	Pea soup
	Cold beef
	Salad, mashed potatoes
	Pheasant

	Macaroni cheese
Tuesday:	Cod and oyster sauce
	Salmi of pheasants
	Stewed beef and vegetables
	Fig pudding
Wednesday:	Ox-tail soup
	Saddle of mutton
	Brussels sprouts, potatoes
	Lemon pudding
Thursday:	Oyster soup
	Cold mutton
	Beetroot, mashed potatoes
	Cabinet pudding
Friday:	Fried sole
	Roast loin of pork
	Greens, potatoes
	Snipe
	Cheese
Saturday:	Mulligatawny soup
	Mutton rissoles, cold pork
	Salad, mashed potatoes
	Cold pudding warmed with wine sauce

An ideal menu to cover the period from Boxing Day to New Year!

To delight the taste-buds of your friends and family, choose your Christmas dishes from this selection of traditional and modern recipes, many of which are over seven centuries old. From the Chicken and Almond Mould, so popular in the fourteenth century, to the Scotch Black Bun, eaten north of the Border at Hogmanay, you can literally recapture the tastes of an old-fashioned Christmas.

Soups

Onion Soup
(Nineteenth century)
Ingredients: 8 medium-sized onions
             3 oz of butter
             1 tablespoon of rice-flour
             1 teaspoon of sugar
             2 quarts of water

Salt and pepper to taste
Butter and flour to thicken

Method: Cut the onions into small pieces. Place in a large saucepan with a little butter, and cook until the onions have softened; mix the rice-flour smoothly with water, add onions, seasoning and sugar, and simmer until tender. Thicken with butter and flour and serve. Delicious served with brown bread and grated cheese sprinkled on the top.

Chestnut Soup
(Twentieth century)
Ingredients: 1 lb of chestnuts
1 oz of butter
1 large onion
1 potato
2 celery sticks
2 pints of stock
Salt and pepper to taste
2 tablespoons of medium sherry
½ pint of white sauce

Method: Chop shelled chestnuts coarsely. Cook onion in a saucepan with butter until soft. Add chestnuts, chopped celery, potatoe and stock – chicken or turkey stock is perfect. Cook until vegetables and chestnuts are tender. Purée in a liquidizer or by rubbing through a sieve. Make a white sauce, add the sherry and chestnut purée, sugar and seasoning, and serve.

Leek Soup
(Fourteenth century)
Ingredients: 6-8 leeks sliced lengthways
½ bottle of white wine
½ pint of stock
6 slices of toasted French bread
2 oz of butter

Method: Place sliced leeks in a saucepan with butter and sauté until tender. Add stock and simmer for forty-five minutes. Season with salt and black pepper. Pour in a tureen, float French bread on the top and serve.

Oxtail Soup
(Eighteenth century)
Ingredients: 3 oxtails
          3 medium onions
          5 cloves
          1 tablespoon of salt
          $\frac{1}{4}$ teaspoon of allspice
          Black pepper

Oxtails can be bought at the butcher's or supermarket and are usually split into joints. Soak oxtails overnight in salt water. The next day put the tails, chopped onions, cloves and allspice in a large saucepan and cover with cold water. Add black pepper and simmer for two hours until the meat is tender. Skim the top off the broth and strain it through a sieve. Chop up the meat, add it to the soup and serve.

Spinach Soup
(Twentieth century)
Ingredients: 1 lb of spinach
          1 oz of butter
          1 small onion
          1 oz of cornflour
          $1\frac{1}{2}$ pints of milk
          4 tablespoons of cream
          2 egg yolks
          Seasoning

Method: Slice onion and cook in butter until soft. Add cornflour dissolved in milk, stir and boil for three minutes. Add cooked, chopped spinach (you can sieve the spinach for a less coarse soup) and milk and bring to the boil. In a bowl, blend the two egg yolks and the cream together, and add to the soup, stirring all the time. Season and serve.

Green Pea Soup
(Nineteenth century)
Ingredients: 8 oz of peas (dried or frozen)
          2 pints of bacon stock
          2 medium onions
          1 carrot
          1 turnip
          1 teaspoon of sugar
          Salt and pepper

76

Method: Soak the peas in the bacon stock, preferably overnight. Chop up the vegetables and add to the soup, with the sugar and seasoning. Bring to the boil and simmer for 1-1½ hours. Serve with pieces of crispy bacon as a garnish.

All the soups, with the exception of the Chestnut Soup, can be made and frozen in containers until needed. Use plastic containers rather than metal, and allow to cool completely before putting in the deep freeze.

Fish

These days we rarely serve a fish course with a Christmas dinner, but after an excess of poultry, fish can make a palatable change during Christmas week, though you'll probably have to use frozen fish.

Suprême of Sole
(Twentieth century)
Ingredients: 4 fillets of sole
1 pint of fish stock (or ½ pint of stock and ½ pint of white wine)
¼ pint of cream
¼ lb of mushrooms
1 small onion
Butter
Mustard
Salt and pepper

Method: Skin the fillets of sole and spread them with a mild mustard, preferably French. Sprinkle with salt and freshly milled black pepper. Starting from the tail, roll the fish up and place in a buttered dish. Pour in the stock, or stock and wine. Chop the onion finely and sprinkle over the top, and add the sliced mushrooms. Add a knob of butter. Cover and bake, gas Mark 3, 325°F, for twenty-five to thirty minutes. Just before serving, place fillets on a serving dish and keep hot. Stir cream into the stock that the fish were cooked in, and blend in two tablespoons of mustard powder. Bring to the boil and serve poured over the fish.

Fish Stock (for the above recipe)
(Fifteenth century)
Ingredients: 2 lbs of fish bones and trimmings
2 pints of water
1 large onion

2 bay leaves
1 carrot
1 teaspoon of dried thyme
Salt and pepper
1 stick of celery

Method: Place all the ingredients together in a large saucepan. Bring to the boil and simmer for thirty minutes. Strain carefully through a sieve, making certain that no small bones end up in the finished stock. This recipe should result in one pint of stock.

Salmon Pie
(Eighteenth century)
Ingredients: 1 lb of salmon
$\frac{1}{2}$ pint of prawns or shrimps
$\frac{1}{2}$ lb of lobster meat
1 teaspoon of salt
$\frac{1}{2}$ teaspoon of pepper
$\frac{1}{2}$ teaspoon of dried thyme
$\frac{1}{2}$ teaspoon of powdered nutmeg
$\frac{1}{2}$ teaspoon of powdered ginger
$\frac{1}{2}$ teaspoon of mace
$\frac{1}{4}$ pint of fish stock
$\frac{1}{4}$ pint of red wine
1 oz of butter
1 teaspoon of lemon juice
$1\frac{1}{2}$ lb of pastry

Method: Line a pie dish with pastry. Cut the salmon into two-inch-thick pieces (about the size of a matchbox) and place a layer in the bottom of the dish. Then add a layer of prawns, followed by a layer of lobster. Add the herbs and spices, and end with a layer of salmon. Pour over the stock and wine. Add the butter in small knobs and pour over the lemon juice and seasoning. Put the pastry crust on top of the pie and bake, gas Mark 5, 375°F, for thirty-five to forty-five minutes until the pastry is golden brown. Serve with creamed mashed potatoes, and cauliflower and peas.

A similar pie can be made using halibut, whiting, sole or bass. Thinly sliced hard-boiled eggs can be added to the pie, too, for variation, along with sliced tomatoes.

Potted Salmon
(Nineteenth century)
A Mrs Beeton favourite
Ingredients: Salmon
Pounded mace
2 bay leaves
$\frac{1}{4}$ lb of butter
Cloves and pepper to taste

Method: Skin the salmon and clean it by wiping it thoroughly with a cloth; cut it into square pieces. Sprinkle with salt. Lay in a dish with the rest of the ingredients and bake. When cooked, drain and press into pots for use. Do not fill the pots completely, but when quite cold pour over it melted butter. This makes an excellent starter if served with slices of brown bread or strips of toast.

Skate with Black Butter
(Twentieth century)
Ingredients: 8 oz of 'wing' of skate per person
2 oz of butter
1 tablespoon of lemon juice
Salt

Method: Using a very sharp knife, scrape away the skin of the fish. This is 'jelly-like' in texture. Melt the butter in a saucepan until it is brown (not black!). Put the fish in a piece of tinfoil and pour the melted butter over the top. Having poured the butter from the pan, immediately put the lemon juice and a pinch of salt in it. Once the juice 'foams', pour that over the fish too. Wrap the fish up in the foil completely and bake for approximately twenty-five minutes, gas Mark 4, 350°F. Skate is a delicious fish with a delicate flavour, and this makes an excellent light lunch dish, perhaps on a day when you know that you are going to have a heavy, rich meal in the evening.

Meat and Poultry

Roast Goose and Sauce Madame
(Fourteenth century)
Ingredients: 1 goose (6–8 lb for 4–6 people)
1 teaspoon of sage
1 teaspoon of thyme

1 teaspoon of parsley
4 tablespoons of quince jelly
5 pears (tinned are ideal)
$\frac{1}{4}$ lb of green grapes (seeded)
$\frac{1}{2}$ pint of stock
$\frac{1}{2}$ pint of red wine
1 teaspoon of nutmeg
1 teaspoon of cinnamon
$\frac{1}{2}$ teaspoon of ginger
1 crushed clove of garlic

Method: Mix together in a bowl the herbs, jelly, fruit and garlic. Blend together and place inside the goose. The neck of the bird needs to be stopped up; this can be done with a large orange with cloves pressed into it, or you can simply sew the flesh together with coarse thread. Roast the goose at fifteen minutes to a pound and fifteen minutes over. Start with a hot oven and then reduce the heat to moderate after half an hour. As the meat is very greasy, there is no need to put any butter or lard on the bird.

When the goose is cooked, spoon out the stuffing from inside the goose and place it in a saucepan with the stock and some of the juices from the bird. Add the spices and bring to the boil. Finally add the red wine (port is an excellent accompaniment too) and simmer the sauce for a few minutes. Serve the sauce with the goose.

Roast Turkey
(Nineteenth century)
Ingredients: 1 turkey
　　　　　　Forcemeat
　　　　　　Butter
　　　　　　Flour

Method: Stuff the turkey with the forcemeat (or make into separate balls and cook around the turkey if you prefer). Rub the breast of the bird well with butter, and baste during cooking. Roast for about $1\frac{1}{2}$ hours for a small bird: two hours for a medium bird of around 10 lb; $2\frac{1}{2}$ hours or longer if larger. On average cook for around fifteen minutes a pound, and fifteen over twenty minutes a pound if cooked in tinfoil. About twenty minutes before serving, sprinkle flour over the bird and then baste. This will help the bird to brown and thicken the juices for gravy.

A duck or chicken can be roasted in exactly the same way.

Roast Sucking Pig
(Seventeenth century)
If you have a large family, a sucking pig of around 12 lb makes sure that everyone gets plenty, and makes an interesting change from turkey!

Ingredients: 1 sucking-pig
6 oz of mixed herbs
½ lb of butter
2 teaspoons of salt
1 teaspoon of black pepper
5 tablespoons of vinegar
4 tablespoons of cranberry sauce
4 tablespoons of apple sauce

Method: Place 4 oz of butter in a frying-pan and sauté the herbs for a few minutes. Season with salt and pepper and empty the mixture into the pig. Place an apple in the opening. Roast at gas Mark 5, 375°F, for 3½-4 hours or until done. Melt remaining butter in a saucepan, add vinegar and fruit, and pour over the pig before serving. Ensure that the meat is well done.

Baked Ham
(Sixteenth century)
It is always useful to have a ham at Christmas. It is useful for entertaining, for a delicious breakfast or a sandwich at suppertime.

Ingredients: 1 ham
Brown sugar
Cloves
Flour

Method: Soak the ham in cold water for at least twelve hours, preferably changing the water once or twice. This gets rid of any excess salt in the pork. Dry the ham carefully. Press cloves into the ham then make a paste with flour and a little water, and coat the meat to keep in the juices. Roast at gas Mark 6, 400°F, for fifteen minutes, then reduce heat to gas Mark 2, 310°F, allowing thirty minutes a pound. When cooked, remove the dough crust and the skin. Cover with brown sugar or honey. If you want the ham to look really professional, score criss-cross squares in the fat with a sharp knife.

Mutton à la braise, with a ragout of chestnuts
(Eighteenth century)
Ingredients: 1 leg of lamb
     8 rashers of bacon
     2 teaspoons of salt
     $\frac{1}{2}$ teaspoon of black pepper
     2 tablespoons of cooking oil
     $\frac{1}{2}$ lb of shelled chestnuts
     1 pint of stock

Method: Brown the lamb very quickly in a frying-pan with the oil. Remove from pan and, with skewers or cocktail sticks, secure the bacon rashers over the joint. Place in a casserole or large saucepan and pour the stock, salt and pepper over the meat. Simmer for two hours. Add the chestnuts and simmer for a further thirty minutes before serving.

The following are perfect for left-overs.

Chicken and Almond Mould
(Fourteenth century)
Ingredients: 5 oz of diced chicken
     6 oz of rice
     $\frac{1}{2}$ pint of milk
     2 oz of ground almonds
     $\frac{1}{2}$ pint of jellied stock
     $\frac{1}{4}$ teaspoon of saffron
     $\frac{1}{2}$ teaspoon of black pepper
     Gelatine

Method: Mix the ground almonds with the milk in a saucepan. Bring to the boil and add the rice. Cook until rice is tender. Drain and leave to get cold. Sauté chicken in butter with the saffron, salt and black pepper. Leave to get cold. Warm the chicken stock and melt gelatine in it. Add the chicken and the rice and mix thoroughly. Allow to cool, and empty into a buttered mould. When set, turn out on a dish and decorate with almonds.

Turkey Mousse
(Eighteenth century)
Ingredients: $\frac{1}{2}$ lb of cooked chicken (minced)
     $\frac{1}{2}$ oz of grated cheese
     3 eggs
     $\frac{1}{2}$ pint of cream
     2 tablespoons of breadcrumbs

$\frac{1}{2}$ teaspoon of nutmeg
Salt and pepper
Toast

Method: Mix the cheese, turkey and breadcrumbs together thoroughly to form a kind of paste. In a separate bowl, beat the eggs and cream together, add nutmeg and seasoning. Finally stir in the turkey mixture. Place fingers of toast in the bottom of a soufflé dish and pour the mixture over it. Bake in a moderate oven at gas Mark 4, 350°F, for twenty-five minutes, or until well risen.

Turkey Rechauffé
(Nineteenth century)
Ingredients: Left-over turkey
4 oz of butter
4 tablespoons of flour
$\frac{1}{2}$ pint of stock
$\frac{1}{2}$ pint of cream
$\frac{1}{2}$ teaspoon of nutmeg

Method: Melt butter in a frying-pan, and add the turkey pieces. Stir in the flour. Add the stock and cream and warm gently, stirring all the time until a smooth sauce has been produced. Add the nutmeg and seasoning. This is a quick and easy dish to prepare, and is delicious served with fresh vegetables, such as parsnips and carrots, that are available at Christmas.

Spicy Chicken
(Fifteenth century)
Ingredients: $1\frac{1}{2}$ lb of cooked chicken, chopped
$\frac{1}{2}$ pint of white wine
3 egg yolks
6 oz of honey
4 oz of sugar
1 teaspoon of grated lemon peel
1 teaspoon of ground cloves
1 oz of raisins

Method: Place the wine and sugar in a saucepan and boil for five to ten minutes to make a syrup. Keep four to five tablespoons of the syrup to one side, and to the saucepan of syrup add the raisins, peel, honey and cloves. Simmer for three minutes. Beat the egg yolks and add them to the syrup, stirring all the time to prevent the mixture curdling. Continue stirring over a low heat and add the chopped chicken. Pour the mixture into a dish. Pour the syrup that you left to one side over the top. Place the whole dish in the refrigerator for at least three hours before serving.

Vegetables

Creamed Celery
(Eighteenth century)
Ingredients: 1 celery heart per person
$\frac{1}{2}$ pint of cream
2 egg yolks
$\frac{1}{2}$ oz of butter
Salt and pepper

Method: Cut the celery hearts into large pieces. Bring to the boil in water, and simmer until tender, but do not overcook them. Drain. Gently warm the cream in a saucepan. Beat the egg yolks in a bowl and add the cream to them, stirring all the time. Add the salt, pepper and butter. Stir in the celery hearts and serve.

Brussels Sprouts
(Nineteenth century)
Ingredients: 8–10 sprouts per person
Salt
Bicarbonate of soda

Method: Wash and clean the sprouts thoroughly. Boil a saucepan of water and add the salt and soda. Place the sprouts in the boiling water and boil quickly, leaving the pan uncovered. Many people have a tendency to overcook sprouts, whereas ten minutes in boiling water is sufficient. A cross made with a sharp knife in the base of each helps them cook quicker. When cooked, drain and place in a tureen. Put a knob of butter and some black pepper on them and serve immediately. Mrs Beeton used to arrange the sprouts on a dish in the shape of a pineapple. They looked pretty, but this is only for people who do not object to cold sprouts!

Carrots
(Nineteenth century)
Ingredients: 1 large or 4 small carrots per person
Sugar

Method: Cut off the green tops, wash and scrape the carrots. If large, divide the carrots lengthwise into four pieces. Put them into a saucepan of boiling water with a tablespoon of sugar, and boil until tender. Serve with a knob of butter.

Peas
(Nineteenth century)
Ingredients: 2 quarts of fresh peas
               3 oz of fresh butter
               6 green onions
               A bunch of parsley
               Flour
               1 dessertspoon of sugar
               1 teaspoon of flour
Method: Place peas (fresh from the deep freezer!) into a saucepan of cold water and bring to the boil. Meanwhile, in a separate saucepan, melt the butter, add the chopped onions, parsley and sugar. Drain the peas and dredge a little flour over them. Add to the butter mixture and stir well until they are well coated, and serve.

Mashed Potatoes
(Nineteenth century)
Ingredients: 1 lb of potatoes (sufficient for 3)
               1 oz of butter (to every pound of potato)
               2 tablespoons of milk (to every pound of potato)
               Salt to taste
               Black pepper
Method: Peel potatoes and boil them in a large pan of boiling salt water. Drain when cooked. Add milk, butter, salt and pepper to the potatoes and stand back over a gentle heat, and beat until light and fluffy.

Roast Potatoes
(Twentieth century)
Ingredients: 1 lb of potatoes
               4 oz of lard
Method: Peel potatoes, and cut into large chunks. Heat the lard in the oven, while you blanch the potatoes in boiling, salted water for five minutes. Drain the potatoes well, and add to the hot fat. Spoon some of the fat over the potatoes so that they brown all over. Cook for about an hour in a hot oven. Alternatively you can place the potatoes around the meat, if you are roasting a joint. This way the

potatoes are flavoured with the meat juices.

Leeks
(Nineteenth century)
Ingredients: 1 large leek per person
               Butter
Method: Leeks are a sadly misused vegetable, usually boiled in salted water and camouflaged in white sauce. The simplest and most delicious way to cook them is to melt some butter in a saucepan and add the leeks. Let them cook gently in the butter until tender. Serve with some of the butter in which they were cooked, sprinkled generously with black pepper and some grated lemon rind.

Baked Onions
(Nineteenth century)
Ingredients: Large onions
               Butter
               Black pepper
Method: Wash the onions, but leave them in their skins. Bake them in the oven for two to three hours just as you would jacket potatoes. (If you boil the onions for five minutes first, this will cut down the cooking time.) When cooked, cut open and serve with butter and pepper. They make an excellent supper dish on their own.

Cauliflower
(Twentieth century)
Ingredients: 1 cauliflower
               3 oz of Gruyère cheese (grated)
               3 oz of butter
Method: Instead of the usual cauliflower in cheese sauce, boil the cauliflower in salted water and, when *just* cooked, place in a fireproof dish, sprinkle the cheese over the cauliflower sprigs and then pour over the melted butter (melt in a saucepan, but do not let it go brown). Place the whole dish under the grill for a few minutes until it bubbles away. Serve.

Forcemeats

Mrs Beeton's Forcemeat
(Nineteenth century)
Ingredients: 2 oz of ham or lean bacon
$\frac{1}{4}$ lb of suet
The rind of half a lemon
1 teaspoon of minced parsley
1 teaspoon of minced herbs
6 oz of breadcrumbs
2 eggs
Salt, pepper and mace to taste

Method: Shred the ham or bacon; chop the suet, lemon peel and herbs, taking care that it is all finely minced; add a seasoning to taste of salt, cayenne and mace, and blend thoroughly with breadcrumbs before wetting. Beat and strain the eggs, work these up with the other ingredients, and the forcemeat is ready for use. When it is made up into balls, fry to a nice brown in boiling lard, or put them on a tin and bake for half-an-hour in a moderate oven. The forcemeat should be of sufficient body to cut with a knife, but not dry and heavy.

Forcemeat Balls
(Eighteenth century)
Ingredients: $\frac{1}{2}$ lb of minced veal
$\frac{1}{2}$ lb of shredded suet
2 egg yolks
2 tablespoons of mixed herbs
$\frac{1}{2}$ teaspoon of mace
1 tablespoon of grated lemon peel

Method: Put all the ingredients together in a bowl and beat into fine pulpy mixture. Dip your hands in flour and roll the mixture into little balls. Either fry until brown or bake in the oven with a few knobs of lard until brown (approx. thirty minutes).

Stuffing for Chicken or Turkey
(Fifteenth century)
Ingredients: 5 hard-boiled egg yolks
4 oz of chopped parsley

2 oz of butter
1 teaspoon of fresh ginger, chopped
½ teaspoon of saffron
Salt and pepper

Method: In the fifteenth century egg yolks were used instead of breadcrumbs, although they unfortunately did not come up with a recipe for a dish using only egg whites! So as not to waste them, chop the whites up and use with chopped fish and rice to make kedgeree. For the stuffing, place all the ingredients in a bowl and blend together. Use the mixture to stuff the chicken.

Stuffing for Goose
(Fifteenth century)
Ingredients: 3–4 rashers of bacon
4 hard-boiled egg yolks
1 medium onion
¼ teaspoon of ground ginger
½ teaspoon of ground cinnamon
¼ teaspoon of saffron
2 crushed cloves
4 oz of butter

Method: Melt the butter in a saucepan. Add the bacon, finely chopped, and the onion, diced. Stir in the rest of the ingredients and stuff the goose with the mixture. Two tablespoons of breadcrumbs can be used in place of the egg yolks if preferred, for a more modern approach.

Celery and Onion Stuffing
(Twentieth century)
Ingredients: 3 sticks of celery
1 small onion
3 oz of breadcrumbs
2 tablespoons of chopped parsley
1 tablespoon of corn oil
1 small egg

Method: Melt the oil, or butter if you prefer, in a pan and gently fry the celery and onion, both chopped very finely until soft. Remove from heat and stir in the remaining ingredients.

Chestnut Stuffing
(Nineteenth century)
Ingredients: 2 lbs of chestnuts (shelled and chopped)
              4 oz of butter
              2 large onions
              8 oz of celery
              4 oz of chopped bacon
              4 oz of breadcrumbs
Method: Melt butter in a saucepan and add chopped onion and celery. Fry gently until soft. Add the bacon, chestnuts, breadcrumbs and seasoning.

Sauces

Chicken Sauce
(Eighteenth century)
Ingredients: $\frac{1}{2}$ lb of cooked chicken livers
              $\frac{3}{4}$ pint of pale ale
              5 oz of pickled cucumbers
              1 tablespoon of flour
Method: Blend the flour with the ale in a saucepan, add the pickles and liver, and heat, stirring all the time. Serve as a gravy.

Mrs Beeton's Brown Gravy
(Nineteenth century)
Ingredients: 2 large onions
              1 large carrot
              2 oz of butter
              3 pints of boiling water
              1 bunch of herbs
              A wineglassful of ale
              Salt and pepper
Method: Slice, flour and fry the onions and carrots in the butter until of a nice light brown colour; then add the boiling water and the remaining ingredients; let the whole stew gently for about an hour; then strain, and when cold, skim off the fat. If thought necessary, thicken with 2 oz of flour.

Bread Sauce
(Nineteenth century)
Ingredients: 1 pint of milk
$\frac{1}{4}$ lb of crumbs (not fresh bread)
1 onion
Pounded mace
1 oz of butter
Salt and pepper to taste

Method: Peel and quarter the onion, and simmer it in milk until perfectly tender. Break the bread, which should be stale, into small pieces; put in a very clean saucepan and strain milk over it, cover it up and let it remain for an hour to soak. Now beat it with a fork very smoothly, and add a seasoning of pounded mace, salt and pepper, with 1 oz of butter; bring the whole mixture to the boil and serve. To enrich this sauce, a small quantity of cream may be added before sending it to the table.

Melted Butter Sauce
(Fifteenth century)
Ingredients: 5 oz of butter
2 oz of flour
1 pint of cold water
Salt and pepper

Method: Over a low heat, melt the butter in a saucepan. Stir in the flour. Cook gently for two to three minutes. Slowly add the water, stirring all the time. Bring to simmering, and lower heat immediately. Add the salt and pepper and the remaining butter in small pieces, beating all the time. Do not allow the sauce to boil at any time. This sauce is delicious served with leeks or asparagus.

Cranberry Sauce
(Eighteenth century)
Ingredients: 12 oz of cranberries
$\frac{1}{4}$ pint of water
3 oz of sugar
$\frac{1}{2}$ oz of butter

Method: Place the sugar and water in a saucepan and bring to the boil. Add the cranberries and cook until a thick sauce results. Add the butter and serve.

Brandy Sauce
(Nineteenth century)
Ingredients: 1 tablespoon of baked flour
              3 oz of fresh butter
              1 tablespoon of moist sugar
              $\frac{3}{4}$ pint of boiling water
              1 wineglassful of brandy
Method: Work the flour and butter together with a wooden spoon, then stir in the boiling water and sugar, boil gently for ten minutes. Add the brandy and serve.

Sabayon Sauce
(Twentieth century)
Ingredients: 1 wineglass of cream sherry
              3 egg yolks
              3 oz of castor sugar
              $\frac{1}{2}$ teaspoonful of vanilla essence
Method: Place the egg yolks, essence and sugar in a bowl, and place this bowl in one of boiling water. Beat the ingredients until smooth. Add the sherry and whisk until the sauce thickens and becomes light and fluffy. It is then ready to serve. For a richer sauce, fold in the three stiffly beaten egg whites just before serving.

Desserts

Buttered Oranges
(Eighteenth century)
Ingredients: $\frac{3}{4}$ pint of fresh orange juice
              4 egg yolks
              2 egg whites
              1 oz of butter
              2 tablespoons of rose water
Method: Beat the eggs and sugar. Continue beating, and add orange juice and rose water. Place the bowl over a saucepan of hot water and beat until the mixture thickens. Add the butter. When the mixture is really thick, transfer it to a soufflé dish and refrigerate for a couple of hours before serving.

Spiced custard
(Fourteenth century)
Ingredients: 6 egg yolks
             4 egg whites
             2 oz of sugar
             1 pint of red wine
             $\frac{1}{2}$ teaspoon of cinnamon, nutmeg, saffron, mace and
             cloves

Method: Heat the wine gently in a saucepan. Whisk in the beaten eggs and spices. Stir over a low heat until the mixture thickens. Turn into a soufflé dish and chill.

Plum Pudding
(Nineteenth century)
Ingredients: 1$\frac{1}{2}$ lbs of raisins
             $\frac{1}{2}$ lb of currants
             $\frac{1}{2}$ lb of mixed peel
             $\frac{3}{4}$ lb of breadcrumbs
             $\frac{3}{4}$ lb of suet
             8 eggs
             1 wineglassful of brandy

Method: Stone and cut the raisins in half, but do not chop them; wash, pick and dry the currants, and mince the suet finely; cut the candied peel into thin slices, and grate down the bread into fine crumbs. When all these dry ingredients are prepared, mix them well together; then moisten the mixture with the eggs, which should be well beaten, and the brandy; stir well, that everything may be very thoroughly blended, and press the pudding into a buttered mould; tie it down tightly with a floured cloth, and boil for five or six hours. The pudding should be made in advance, and the day it is to be eaten it should be boiled for at least two hours. Turn out of the mould, pour a wineglassful of brandy around the pudding and light it. Serve with brandy sauce.

Duke of Buckingham's Pudding
(Eighteenth century)
Ingredients: 1 lb of shredded suet
             4 oz of raisins
             2 eggs
             $\frac{1}{2}$ teaspoon of nutmeg
             $\frac{1}{4}$ teaspoon of ginger

4 oz of sugar
2 oz of flour

Method: Blend all the ingredients together. Put in a buttered dish, cover with a cloth and boil for three hours.

Serve with sauce: 2 tablespoons of sugar
                    2 tablespoons of butter
                    2 tablespoons of sherry

Warm together in a saucepan and pour over the sauce before serving.

Mince Pies
(Nineteenth century)
Ingredients: Mincemeat
              Puff pastry
              The white of an egg

Method: Take some good puff pastry and roll it out to the thickness of about a quarter of an inch, and line some good-sized patty pans with it; fill them with mincemeat, cover with the pastry and cut it off all around close to the edge of the tin. Put the pies in a brisk oven and bake for twenty-five minutes. For a glazed look, paint with egg white before cooking. Or, if you prefer, when cooked sprinkle with powdered sugar. Mince pies can be reheated at any time by popping them in the oven for about ten minutes, and they will be as good as if freshly made.

Christmas Miscellany

Puff Pastry for Mince Pies
(Nineteenth century)
Ingredients: 8 oz of self-raising flour
              5 oz of lard
              $\frac{1}{2}$ teaspoon of salt
              $\frac{1}{4}$ pint of cold water

Method: Place flour and salt in a bowl. Cut fat into small squares and stir into the flour with a knife. (Do NOT rub in.) Adding a little cold water at a time, mix to a stiff paste. With floured hands, lift out onto a floured surface and roll out into a strip. Fold it into three. Turn one of the open ends towards you and roll out again. Do this three times. Leave for fifteen minutes before using.

Christmas Tree Biscuits
(Twentieth century)
Ingredients: 8 oz of plain flour
6 oz of butter
5 oz of castor sugar
2 oz of semolina
1 egg yolk mixed with 2 dessertspoons of cold water
1 oz of currants

Method: Put flour in a bowl and rub in the butter. Add sugar, semolina and currants. Mix to a dough with egg and water. Roll out on a floured surface and cut out Christmas tree shapes. Bake for ten minutes at gas Mark 6, 400°F. When cold, spread tree part with jam and sprinkle with desiccated coconut.

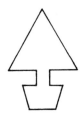

Lady Crabtree's Christmas Cake
(Twentieth century)
Ingredients: 4 oz of butter
4 oz of demerara sugar
3 eggs
$\frac{1}{2}$ lb of currants
$\frac{1}{4}$ lb of sultanas
2 oz of mixed peel
2 oz of raisins
1 oz of chopped almonds
6 oz of self-raising flour
Pinch of salt
3 tablespoons of brandy
1 tablespoon of cream sherry

Method: Cream butter and sugar; add eggs one at a time. Add all other ingredients, brandy last. Fold in the flour with a metal spoon. Treble line cake tin with brown paper and greaseproof paper. Bake in pre-heated oven gas Mark 2, 300°F, for at least four hours.

When cake is turning brown, place a sheet of greaseproof paper over the top. When cooked and cool, prick the top and pour further brandy over it. For a more spicy cake include:

> 1 teaspoonful of cinnamon
> 1 teaspoonful of mixed spice
> 1 teaspoonful of nutmeg
> $\frac{1}{2}$ teaspoonful of ginger

Almond Paste
(Twentieth century)
Ingredients: 12 oz of ground almonds
> 6 oz of castor sugar
> 6 oz of icing sugar
> $\frac{1}{2}$ teaspoon of lemon juice
> Almond essence
> A little sherry or rum
> 3 egg yolks
> Apricot jam

Method: Mix the ground almonds, castor sugar and icing sugar in a bowl. Whisk the egg yolks, and whisk in the lemon juice, almond essence and sherry or rum. Pour the liquid into the dry mixture and mix together to make a paste. Knead with the hand until smooth. Roll out the paste into a round large enough to cover the top of the cake, and a strip wide enough and long enough to go round the side. Spread the apricot jam lightly over the surface of the cake before putting on the almond paste: the jam will help it to adhere to the surface.

Royal Icing
(Twentieth century)
Ingredients: 2 lb of icing sugar
> 4 egg whites
> 2 teaspoons of lemon juice
> (Sufficient for a 9-inch cake)

Method: Beat egg whites and lemon juice together. Add half the sieved icing sugar to the egg whites and beat well. Add the rest of the sugar gradually, until the icing is stiff and stands up in peaks.

Scotch Black Bun
(Traditional)
Ingredients: Pastry – 12 oz of flour
$\frac{3}{4}$ teaspoon of baking powder
6 oz of lard
2 oz of sugar
Water
Egg white to glaze
Filling: 8 oz of sugar
4 lb of mixed dried fruit
4 oz of mixed peel
8 oz of chopped almonds
1 lb of flour
$1\frac{1}{2}$ oz of mixed spice
2 eggs
$\frac{1}{2}$ oz of bicarbonate of soda
$\frac{1}{2}$ oz of cream of tartar

Method: Make the pastry by putting flour, sugar and baking powder into a bowl, rub in the lard and make into a stiff paste with the water. Turn onto a floured board and roll out. Line a buttered nine-inch tin with the pastry, leaving enough for the top. For the filling, put all the ingredients in a large bowl and blend together thoroughly. Fill the pastry case, and cover with the remaining pastry. Brush with egg white and bake in a moderate oven, gas Mark 3, 325°F, for two hours, then turn down to gas Mark 2, 300°F, for a further hour.

Christmas Drinks

Nothing is nicer, or more warming, than a glass of traditional hot punch or mulled wine at Christmas. As you give a toast at your parties, greet everybody with the cry 'Waes hael!', which is Anglo-Saxon for 'Be well!' From it, of course, has derived the word 'wassail', and if you feel like a spot of wassailing, grab your wassail bowl and fill it with one of the following!

Hot Punch
(Traditional)
Ingredients: $\frac{1}{2}$ pint of rum
$\frac{1}{2}$ pint of brandy
$\frac{1}{4}$ lb of sugar

                    1 large lemon
                    ½ teaspoonful of nutmeg
                    1 pint of boiling water

Method: Rub the sugar over the lemon until it has absorbed all the yellow part of the skin, then put the sugar into a punchbowl; add the lemon juice (free from pips), and mix these two ingredients well together. Pour over them the boiling water, stir well together, add the rum, brandy and nutmeg; mix thoroughly and the punch will be ready to serve. It is very important in making good punch that all the ingredients are thoroughly incorporated, and to ensure success, the processes of mixing must be diligently attended to. Allow a quart for four people.

Mulled Wine
(Nineteenth century)
Ingredients: To every pint of wine allow one large cupful of water, sugar and spice to taste.

Method: In making preparations like the above, it is very difficult to give the exact proportions of ingredients such as sugar and spice, as what quantity might suit one person would to another be quite distasteful. Boil the spice in the water until the flavour is extracted, then add the wine and sugar, and bring the whole almost to boiling point. Then serve with strips of crisp dry toast, or with biscuits. The spices usually used for mulled wine are cloves, grated nutmeg and cinnamon or mace. Any kind of wine may be mulled, but port and claret are those usually selected for the purpose, and the latter requires a very large proportion of sugar. The vessel that the wine is boiled in must be delicately clean and should be kept exclusively for the purpose. Small tin warmers may be purchased for a trifle, which are more suitable than saucepans, as, if the latter are not scrupulously clean, they will spoil the wine, by imparting to it a very disagreeable flavour. These warmers should be used for no other purpose.

Posset Cup
(Nineteenth century)
Ingredients: 1 pint of milk
                     ⅓ pint of sherry
                     ⅓ pint of ale
                     4 teaspoons of sugar

Method: Heat the milk in a saucepan almost to boiling point. Put the sherry, ale and sugar in a jug and pour on the milk. Serve immediately with a sprinkling of nutmeg on the top.

Irish Coffee
(Traditional)
Ingredients: Hot fresh coffee
              Fresh cream
              Sugar to taste
              1 measure of Irish whiskey

Method: Percolate fresh coffee. Using special Irish coffee glasses, or any glass that is heat-proof, fill two-thirds full of black coffee. Stir in a spoonful or two of sugar, according to taste. Add a measure of whiskey, then gently pour fresh cream over the back of a warm spoon so that it floats on top of the coffee. Don't stir it! Sip the coffee through the cream.

WHAT CAN I
GIVE HIM?

THE ORIGINS OF CHRISTMAS PRESENTS

The climax of Christmas for most of us must surely be the giving and receiving of presents. For children, who are relieved of the headache of actually buying gifts, it is a time of sublime anticipation and pure joy to wake on Christmas morning and see the presents at the foot of the bed. The giving of presents at this time has been a custom that has quite naturally lingered through the ages from the Saturnalia and Kalends celebrations when garlands of flowers, candles and dolls were presented as symbolic gifts to bring good luck and prosperity for the future. Although the early Christian Church turned its nose up at pagan rituals, its members soon saw that they were missing out on present-giving and cleverly decided to adopt the practice in remembrance of the gifts brought to the infant Jesus by the kings and the shepherds.

Today children in Britain, or young children at least, expect their presents to come from Father Christmas, to whom they have usually written a letter well in advance. This is a practice that all parents should encourage, because a letter like this provides a clear indication of what the child wants, and as long as the demands are reasonable, it is fun to adhere to them and so prolong the child's belief in Father Christmas for as long as possible. If, however, your daughter writes: 'Dear Santa, please can I have a big doll, a new bike and my violin busted,' as one child actually wrote, discretion is obviously the key word! In days of coal fires children used to write their letter and then burn it. Heaven knows how they thought Santa was going to read it. Katie in *What Katie Did* had a little more intelligence and created a draught so that the letter actually flew up the chimney, where presumably she thought Santa would find it on the way down. Modern children do not have such worries, and if you are stuck for what to buy your child, get him or her to write a letter and then offer to post it to the North Pole, where Father Christmas lives, of course, and then you will have it as a source of reference!

Father Christmas's gift-bearing persona has evolved over the centuries and is a mixture of the benevolent old St Nicholas and the pagan god Odin the Gift-Bringer who was said to ride across the midnight sky in December and punish the wicked and reward the good. He rode in a horse-drawn sleigh, which by nineteenth-century American intervention and imagination became reindeer-drawn. Now the familiar rosy-cheeked Father Christmas, the athletic climber of chimneys, resident of Selfridge's (one American store has five Santas to stop children queueing!) and descendant of Odin is as essential a part of Christmas in Britain as the icing on the Christmas cake.

Other countries have their own ideas, of course. A beautiful girl with a crown of lighted candles called Christkindl delivers gifts to German children. She is the messenger of the Christ Child and, although she doesn't come down chimneys, she can walk through locked doors. Traditionally a room in the house is locked up so that no one can enter it. Then at midnight on Christmas Eve parents wake up their children, and together they all go down and unlock the door, only to discover that clever old Christkindl has mysteriously left presents for all of them. Sometimes she has even lit a fire and the candles on the Christmas tree too!

In many Scandinavian countries a friendly gnome, a miniature Santa Claus, called Julenisse, delivers the presents during the night. Just as British children often leave a mince pie and a glass of milk for Santa, and possibly something for the reindeer too, Scandinavian children leave Julenisse a bowl of porridge. Everyone to their own taste. Russian children's presents arrive via one Grandfather Frost: Spanish children's are delivered by the Three Kings on camels, and in Italy a witch known as La Befana is the Christmas figure whom children watch and wait for. They have to wait, too, because La Befana brings their presents on Twelfth Night rather than Christmas Day.

THE RULES OF PRESENT GIVING

There is an old adage which says that it is far better to give than to receive. To some this is true, but to many it is an idealized sentiment. Nevertheless, receiving a present can be pretty horrendous: often it is embarrassing trying to look pleased and grateful for a gift that you do not like, will never use and can't wait to go and change as soon as the shops open again after their Christmas break. Worse still, you usually have to write and thank the giver for it and say how much you've always wanted a *diamanté* teapot stand or a real badger-hair shaving brush. Nevertheless, the actual receiving of the present required little effort on your part; it is the giving of a present that causes the real headache. Choosing, buying, wrapping and presenting Christmas gifts take up an awful lot of time, energy and money, three luxuries that few people have during the approach to Christmas. Year after year it has to be faced, and still it doesn't get any easier.

There is, however, a definite art to giving Christmas presents and once you've mastered it, life will look a lot less grim. Here are the TEN GOLDEN RULES of successful gift giving:

Rule 1
Buy as You Would be Bought For
This does not mean that you should only buy things for other people that you would like to have yourself; it means buy things for others in the spirit in which you hope they would buy things for you. Choose presents that you know the receiver will appreciate and, even if it is not to your taste, get something that is *worthy* of you.

Rule 2
Keep a Present List
To save time and trauma, and to prevent giving the same person the same present two years running, it is essential to keep a list. An exercise book is ideal because it is unlikely to get lost. Simply list the recipients' names down the left-hand side of the page, and the year at the top. You can then see at a glance exactly what you have given each person each year if you list the presents as you buy them, and during Christmas shopping you can keep a tally of how many you have bought and how many are still left to buy. If you want a really accurate record, jot down what you were given as well. It's not such a mammoth job as it's only done once a year, and it helps when writing those interminable 'thank you' letters too, for you can write to Auntie Mabel and say how grateful you are for the tea-towels, which will be so useful in drying up the coffee mugs that you received last year. Your list should be set out like this:

	19-1		19-2	
	Given	Received	G	R
MOTHER	Slippers	Necklace	Brooch	Perfume
FATHER	Dressing-gown	Perfume	Books	Hair dryer
GRANDMA	Perfume	China	Vase	Glass
AUNTIE GWEN	Notelets	Slippers	Mirror	Magazine Subscription
AUNTIE EILEEN	Camera	Cassettes	Slide Box	Clock
JOE	Socks	Chocolates	After Shave	Book Token
MILLICENT	Earrings	Flying Ducks	Make-Up	Earmuffs

Rule 3

Do Not Give Away Last Year's Gifts

However much you may dislike one of your presents, don't keep it for a year and then give it to someone else – unless it's to someone you don't like! Second-hand gifts always have that tell-tale bottom-drawer staleness, however carefully you've kept them. There's also that terrible danger that you might give it back to the person who gave it to you, or give it to someone who was with the person who bought it for you when they bought it, or even more alarming that the donor might call and see you and expect to see their gift in use. Why aren't those flying ducks adorning your wall? You can always say that you treasure them too much to have them out all the time, but it's not a wise move. No matter how safe you feel you may be in giving away last year's presents, be sure your sins will find you out.

Rule 4

Spread Your Christmas Shopping Through the Year

Yes, every year we have at least 295 days in which to do Christmas shopping! Not that you should spend all year continually buying presents, but do bear Christmas in mind, and if you see something suitable for someone, *get it.* Don't worry because it's only the middle of May or the end of September, get it while you think about it. Leave it until December and the chances are that what you had in mind will either be gone or more expensive or it will have slipped your mind altogether. Buying presents during the year prevents a frantic panic in the crowded December shops.

Rule 5

Never Ask What People Want Unless You're Prepared to Buy It

You might be stuck for an idea for what to buy Uncle Ernie this year, but if you *ask* him what he wants it might turn out to be something that is difficult to get and costs more money than you intended to spend, and having asked what he wants, you've committed yourself to giving it to him. As human nature goes, if you do get what is asked for, the chances are very high that it will not be *quite* what the person wanted. How often have you heard, 'Yes, it's very nice, but I would have preferred a blue one,' or 'Oh, I've seen them in the shops a little bit larger than this,' and so on. Don't ask, and you won't get into trouble.

Rule 6
Be Tactful in Your Buying
Don't give a deodorant to someone with a personal problem, or the 'F-Plan Diet' to someone who is slightly overweight; they might think that you are dropping them a big hint, and it could be painful. Take care when buying for someone recently bereaved, also. You don't want to get something that brings back painful memories of the departed, nor should you try to be too bright and give a year's subscription to an Escort Agency.

Rule 7
Do Not Buy 'Improving' Gifts
Christmas is not the time to try to change people, and even if your neighbour does wear shocking pink lipstick, this is not the time to try to improve her by buying a dark cherry one. If Cousin Walter enjoys reading books of graffiti, buy graffiti books, not the Complete Works of Thomas Hardy. Only buy an improving gift if you know the person really well and know that they are going to appreciate it. An English teacher might not be happy or feel improved by being given a dictionary of everyday spellings, but a teenager studying 'O' level English might.

Rule 8
Remember that People Age
Christmas is often a time for contacting people whom we don't see throughout the rest of the year, and often the contact is by mail. It is easy to forget that people age and that children grow up. In your mind your godson in Aberdeen might still be playing with toy cars, but when you add up the years since you last saw him, he could easily be driving his own. It may seem like yesterday that Auntie Alice used to go pot-holing, but that was ten years ago and she's now in retirement due to arthritis. Christmases come quickly, and so do the years.

Rule 9
Don't Be Too Generous
As long as you have the money and can afford it, it would seem impossible to be too generous to someone, but it's not. The more money you have, the more thoughtful and less extravagant you must be, otherwise it can be acutely embarrassing for the recipient. It may seem like a lovely idea to give your nephew a television and video-recorder to take to university with him, but if his parents can only afford to give him a portable radio, it would make their gift lose its significance. It can be easy to go the other way too and buy something that is more expensive than you can afford. It's so easy to be tempted to give beyond your means at Christmas, but don't. It's embarrassing to receive a beautiful gift from someone when you know that they can't really afford it.

Rule 10
Remove the Price
Unless you want someone to know that you've spent £19.99 on them, or whatever, always remove the price tags from gifts and never ever give them in a shop bag, even if there is wrapping paper on the outside and a Harrods bag on the inside. Don't do it. Christmas is not a time for snobbery and keeping up with the Joneses, but a time of peace and goodwill. However small or inexpensive the gift was, always wrap it up smartly and with care. Whatever the present, it's the thought that counts, so show that there has been some thought put into your gift.

Make a mental note of the Ten Golden Rules before you go shopping and you are well on the way to getting gifts that people are really going to appreciate. The only problem now is *what* to buy! Only you know the people concerned, the kind of merchandise available and what you want to spend – each to his own – but here's a general guideline to the kind of present that will appeal to the various age-ranges:

0 to 3 years old
Buying Christmas gifts for a baby or toddler would seem at first thought like an easy task. After all, they're too young to speak and have no experience of money to place a value on anything, and are usually just as happy sucking away on an old rag doll as playing

with expensive toys. With this age group, however, it is not the baby you have to impress but *the parents*! To them their infant is the most beautiful in the world, and they are not happy with any old thing for their son or daughter. The simplest guideline to buying gifts for this age range is 'squeak, rattle or roll', and any toy that does one or all of those will be adored by any child. Make sure that the toy you buy complies with British safety standards and has no sharp edges or pointed corners. The last thing you want to be blamed for is a baby swallowing your present or being poisoned by toxic paint, so bear that in mind. Here is the kind of gift you should be searching for:

1. Anything that makes a noise, dolls that squeak, bears that growl, rattles, xylophones. Items that drive parents mad after a while, but children love!

2. Anything soft and cuddly. Teddy bears, dogs, pandas, glove puppets and any other lovable stuffed toy that a child can adopt.

3 Practical presents. When a baby is quite new, no parent will mind being showered with gifts like a dozen nappies, feeding cups, bibs, nursery equipment, baby powders and lotions, even a mini-hamper containing tinned baby foods and rusks for a baby who is embarking on solids are all acceptable.

4. Something treasurable. If it is a child's first Christmas, it is not extravagant to give a lasting gift, from a silver knife, fork and spoon set to a Bible and prayer book. An engraved cup, having the child's first shoe silver-plated or buying a few Premium Bonds in the child's name are all good ideas. Even £5 in a Building Society account would be a start.

5. Bath toys, squeaky ducks and floating soap dishes that make bath-time fun for a toddler. Avoid giving bubble baths, although they seem like fun; some parents can be paranoid, and if a child gets a rash or some soap in its eye, you could get the blame!

6. Anything that bounces, such as balls and rubber toys, and those rotund figures that always right themselves when you push them over, are always firm favourites.

7. Large building bricks made of wood or plastic, for building towers that can be knocked over, are always fun. For a young baby

bricks made of foam are available that are completely harmless, even when thrown across the room!

8. Brightly coloured picture books made of cloth or very thick card are popular too, but for the under-threes avoid colouring books or crayons as the child will cause nothing but havoc with them.

4 to 6 years old

A much easier age range to cater for because the child is now fully alert, potty trained and able to speak. If you know the child well, you will already see firm signs of character development, and there will be lots of little budding nurses and engine-drivers. When they get to this age, anything that makes a noise should be avoided altogether, otherwise parents will have a nervous breakdown before Boxing Day. Little Johnny may love the imitation automatic rifle and laser gun that make realistic sounds, but you will not be the most popular person in the world if you give him one! At this age, if it moves, comes to pieces or needs some kind of investigation, you can't go far wrong! It helps to know the child, but here is a basic list of the kind of gift that will be acceptable:

1. Colouring books. This is the age when watercolour paints, non-toxic crayons and pencils are perfect gifts. By now the child knows how to use them and has learnt the meaning of the word 'No!' if he or she decides to draw on the wall or paint the cat. Picture books are inexpensive, and as the child is now at the play-school or infant-school stage, anything that is educational and fun will be perfect.

2. Plastic or wooden alphabets. Many shops sell three-dimensional letters, or sometimes cards with letters on them. These can be used in play but help children to get to know the alphabet and spell out simple words (even if it's only their name) at an age when they will be learning to read and write.

3. Blackboard and chalks. A miniature blackboard is always a firm favourite for drawing, writing and scribbling on, and at an age when children love to 'pretend', they can play at being a teacher.

4. Dressing-up clothes. Children have fertile imaginations and love nothing better than dressing up and pretending to be other

people. If you are not adept with a needle, you can always buy a toy nurse's uniform, a Spiderman outfit or a space suit. There is also an excellent range of children's make-up available that washes off clothes, come off little faces with ease and saves on mother's expensive lipstick.

5. Games and puzzles. Today boxed games state which age-group they are aimed at, so look for one suitable for four- to six-year-olds and you can't go wrong. If it is an only child a jigsaw puzzle will be appreciated, but don't go for five-thousand-piece sets; a simple wooden one will bring hours of amusement, especially if brightly coloured or of favourite TV puppets. Wooden jigsaws are not too easy to find these days but are certainly worth the effort of seeking.

6. Puppets. Much more exciting than dolls because the child can actually use them to create something with a life of their own. Choose a glove-puppet rather than stringed, and if it's of a favourite TV character, it will be loved all the more.

7. Toy tea-sets and utensils. This is the age of 'Let's pretend', and boys and girls alike love to be able to emulate Mummy and Daddy and have real tea-parties, and play with miniature cookers and pots and pans. This is good training for getting them involved in simple household tasks, too.

8. Anything on wheels. Lorries, sports cars, wheelbarrows and animals on wheels will all capture the imagination.

7 to 10 years old
An age when children really do begin to take notice of what you've given them, and its *value*. It is nothing for a freckled nose to be turned up and a pigtailed head tossed because one child has received something bigger and better than another. If giving presents to more than one child in the same family, make sure you treat them equally, and even if the presents don't cost exactly the same, make certain that they *look* as if they do. Here are a few ideas:

1. Cars and dolls. Most children collect something, and they can never have too many dolls or cars. Don't be afraid to give dolls to little boys, because they love playing with them (sometimes even

108

more than little girls). Sex equality applies just as much to children. If you're frightened of the outcome, give a soldier doll to either a boy or a girl and you can't go wrong.

2. Collecting sets. Every child should have a hobby, and if you can start them off collecting stamps, postcards, coins, matchboxes, train-numbers, costume dolls or whatever, you may have given a gift that will bring a lifetime's pleasure. Her Majesty the Queen has been collecting stamps since she was a girl, and since she appears on them she has more incentive than most, but a hobby begun in childhood can continue through adulthood too, and by creating an interest in something now, you might even spark off something that will influence the child's future career.

3. Things to make. Little fingers are itching to do things at this age and can be kept occupied for hours with a kilo of modelling clay, a do-it-yourself kit of the Empire State Building, a cardboard cut-out model theatre or a space-monster that needs putting together. Don't go for anything too ambitious, though.

4. Books and comics. Go for something that is fun, be it a book of cartoons, a joke book or a book of silly poems. A child's version of *Pilgrim's Progress* might impress the parents, but you'll only be looked upon as a bore by their offspring. However intellectual the parents may try to make their children, go for something that will amuse.

5. A magic set. For some reason children of this age love to perform conjuring tricks. It's an age when they want to look big and impress, and being able to perform simple magic tricks really boosts their egos and makes them unbearable when they will keep making eggs appear from nowhere, but they love it. It is a time when they enjoy jokes and novelties too, from whoopee cushions to collapsing teaspoons.

6. A personalized gift. A key ring, a mug, a tee-shirt, absolutely anything that has the child's name printed on it will bring a sparkle to their eyes. Today you can have a name printed on almost anything, even story-books in which the child's name appears throughout, and it's a gift that is very personal and shows that you really have made some effort.

7. Chocolates and sweets. Children don't worry about their figures, and as long as the child isn't a future candidate for weight-watchers or heading for false teeth, no one can object to sweets at Christmas. A large selection of inexpensive sweets will be appreciated far more than an extravagantly dear box of chocolates. Buy the kind of fizzy, mind-blowing sweets that only children like, too, so that they don't feel obliged to share them with adults.

8. Money. Yes, by the age of ten children will go to the ends of the earth and back for 5p, so a piggy-bank with 100 new pennies in will be an exciting gift. At this age quantity seems more important than value so, unless you are going to give a pile of pound coins, give your gift in small change; it seems much more exciting.

11 to 16 years old

Children grow up faster than ever before, and with puberty approaching after mixed infants, the teenagers have disappeared and we are faced with young adults instead, who are often far more worldly wise than parents realize. This is a sensitive time, so choose your present carefully to please both parents and offspring. Don't try to be sophisticated by giving your twelve-year-old niece a see-through nightie, or an illustrated sex-manual to your eleven-year-old godson. However adult they may seem, act with a little dignity!

1. Record or cassette token. Unless you know the person well, it is better to give a token so that they can choose their own gift, rather than to buy an actual record or tape. They not only have the pleasure of receiving your gift but then have the thrill of choosing something that they want. Even if you knew a child's favourite pop group in November, it could easily have changed by Christmas.

2. Pop posters. Teenagers love to decorate their bedrooms with pictures of their idols, and if you know that someone is crazy about Boy George, they will be delighted with a poster. But do have a sneaky look in their bedrooms first, otherwise you could duplicate something. For an extra special gift, write to a pop star well in advance (enclosing a stamped addressed envelope) and see if you can get an autographed photograph. You really will be a hero then!

3. Books. A book or a book token is always acceptable, but it helps to know their interests first. Nothing too heavy and nothing that appears too academic. For girls try books on fashion, make-up or horses. For boys, try anything on fitness (they may not be sporty types, but everyone likes to know about keeping fit), photography or films and you will appeal to most.

4. Smellies! After a boy's first shave, it is a great thrill to be able to splash on after shave! For either sex deodorants, talcum powders, soaps (the novelty kind), foam baths and body lotions will come in useful.

5. A second-hand typewriter, television set or music centre. At this age the fact that something is second-hand will not worry them, and it will be easier on your pocket. They will no doubt have a colour television and video in the lounge, but there's nothing like disappearing to your bedroom with friends and watching what you want to watch, not what stuffy old parents want to see.

6. Science/biology sets. From making simple crystals to creating your own computer programme, anything practical will prove stimulating and enjoyable.

7. A magazine subscription. If you know that they are an avid reader of *Pop World*, *Video Scenes* or *Trollope Weekly*, get them a year's subscription. If they are not magazine lovers, try making them a member of the National Trust so that they can visit stately homes, or a society in which they have an interest.

8. Money. At this age they're usually saving to buy a car, a computer, a horse, or a house, and you don't have to worry about giving pennies. Now they'll take a cheque.

18 to 80 years old
If you are buying for a close relation, a husband, wife or life-long friend, you will know their tastes, and hopefully they will have dropped a few subtle hints as to what they want. But if you're giving a gift to someone that you don't know quite so well, here are a few ideas that usually go down well:

1. A book, record or gift token. This saves you the worry of what to buy and passes the buck on to them.

2. Chocolate liqueurs or, if they are teetotal, a box of very expensive chocolates or after-dinner mints.

3. A bottle of champagne. Even a quarter bottle is an acceptable present because it is a little luxury that people do not usually buy themselves.

4. A plant. You can't go wrong buying a beautiful pot plant, but if you know that they haven't got green fingers, buy one that is hardy!

5. A novelty item. If you know that the person has a sense of humour and you have a good relationship with them, get some witty underwear, a saucy apron or a cushion in the shape of a pair of lips.

6. Something antique. It doesn't have to be enormously costly, but anything Georgian, Victorian or Edwardian that is slightly unusual will cause great delight. Even if they have a house full of Habitat furniture, something antique always fits in, and there are hundreds of shops full of reasonably priced Victoriana these days.

7. A sponge bag, filled with expensive soap, an embroidered face flannel and possibly a small but extravagant hand towel. Items like these are always useful, but only give them to someone who looks as if they don't need them!

8. A practical but unusual gift. A porcelain cream jug, pottery cufflinks, a Welsh stone paperweight, a cut-glass vase, some wine glasses with the family coat of arms engraved on them, a silver photo frame, a Scottish tartan rug, an Irish linen tablecloth, a tapestry purse or bag, a velvet tissue box cover, and so on.

81+ years old

Often the most difficult age to buy for because they've usually had everything, seen everything, done everything and got all they want. And who can blame them? But you're never too old to learn, and books, especially books about life when they were young, are always popular. Lots of pictures and large print if eyesight is failing! One of those discreet page-magnifiers is always a useful gift, and most opticians sell them. A bottle of sherry, port or brandy always goes down well, as do chocolates (soft centres, please!). Senior citizens are often delighted with anything that you have made yourself, too: some home-made coconut ice, a rich fruit cake or a pair of knitted leg-warmers. Treat them with respect and make them feel young at heart, and you'll be very popular.

Wrapping Gifts

This can be a tiresome task, but if you wrap presents as and when you buy them, you can save yourself the task of being faced with a mountain of presents as daunting as Everest. If you haven't the discipline to do this, make the task easier by getting friends and relations to assist you, as long as they don't see their own presents! If one chooses the paper, cuts the sellotape and ribbons, another wraps and seals the parcels, and the last person writes out the gift tags, you can get through the job in no time.

Wrapping-paper can be very expensive. If you've been thrifty, you will have kept the best of last year's paper and use it to wrap smaller presents this year. The best paper to buy is crêpe paper. It is inexpensive and malleable so that it makes even the most awkwardly shaped objects easier to wrap, and if you finish off the parcels with contrasting ribbons and bows, they look very attractive and expensive too.

An easier way to wrap presents is to put them in small boxes. Keep all the boxes you can lay your hands on, and either cover them with coloured paper or spray them with gold or silver paint, and you have an attractive gift box. Pop the present inside, and pack the box with tissue paper if necessary to stop it moving around. Stick down the box with a piece of sticky tape, or tie a ribbon around it, and your present is ready for presenting.

Gift tags can be made easily by cutting them out of last year's Christmas cards (use pinking shears to give you a fancy edge). Punch a hole in them and tie a ribbon through, and you have a simple gift tag. Alternatively you can press a holly leaf, stick it on to a small card and varnish it. This makes a very attractive tag.

Making your own Presents

One way of solving the headache of buying Christmas presents is to make the gifts yourself. With patience, care and a little imagination they needn't look home-made at all and will be treasured for years to come by the recipients.

Scrabble Bag

A Scrabble set is an enjoyable gift for any age group, and to make it a little bit more personal you can make a neat little drawstring bag in which to keep the letters. Use a nice piece of material such as a rich piece of velvet, and cut it into an oblong, twice the length you want the bag to be. Bring the two smallest ends of the bag together. Pin the longest sides and stitch them up to make a bag with the reverse side of the cloth facing you. Make a half-inch hem at the top so that a drawstring can be threaded through. Put in your string and turn the bag inside out so that your stitching is on the inside and you have an excellent pouch in which to keep the letters. If you are really handy with a needle, you can embroider a design or the person's name on the bag.

Herbal Wardrobe Freshener

In the autumn gather some herbs and strong-scented flower seeds, and leaves such as lavender and geranium. Let them dry and then crush them. Make a little bag out of muslin and fill it with the herbs. Tie a ribbon tightly around the neck of the bag, and it is ready to hang in a wardrobe or be placed in a drawer to give off its beautiful aroma. An attractive gift is to make several in different colours. Place them in a polythene bag and seal it so that they retain their smell.

Bottled Snowstorm

This is a gift that will fascinate any child. Find a small, clear bottle with a wide neck and a screw top. A small jamjar would do just as well. Choose the scene that you want to put in the bottle. Cake decorations of snowmen, Santa Claus, reindeer and Christmas trees are ideal, but if you are really adept, you could make a little log cabin or church out of matchsticks. Using tweezers and some strong glue, stick your scene in place inside the bottle and leave it to dry. Make sure the glue is waterproof! Put some desiccated coconut in the bottom of the bottle and fill it up with clear vinegar. Glue the top of the bottle on tightly. When you shake the bottle, there will be a snowstorm inside.

Giant Doll

If you are making a gift for a child of any age (even if she's thirty-nine!), a giant doll is always a firm favourite, and so easy to make. Take a large piece of material, preferably pink (cotton or muslin is ideal) or at least flesh-coloured (and you may like to make a doll of any nationality), and fold the material in half. With a marker pen draw the outline of your doll – it needs to be only very basic:

Cut out the shape through *both* layers of material so that you have two identical pieces. Stitch them carefully with backstitch or a double stitch all the way around the edge, leaving the top of the head open. Turn the whole thing inside out and you have the floppy skin of a doll which you can now stuff with foam pieces, kapok or old tights. When you are happy with the result, stitch up the opening at the top of the head. With odd scraps of material or old baby clothes you can dress the doll. Wool can be sewn to the head to give the doll hair, which can easily be plaited and given ribbons. Buttons can be sewn on for eyes, or a face can be painted on with non-toxic inks if it is for a young child. In fact you can let your imagination run riot. There is no end to the kind of doll that can be produced, or the type of materials you can use. Fur fabric can be bought very cheaply and is ideal for making teddy bears, dogs, rabbits etc.

Giant Cushions
These can be made in exactly the same way as the doll. Cut out two identical shapes, stitch them together and stuff – it's as simple as that! For someone you love, make a giant red heart-shaped cushion out of red velvet. Any cushion can be embellished with ribbons, lace or braid or suit your own design. Pet cushions are fun to create too. Use a fairly tough material, and one that is spongeable. Cut

115

out two large squares (depending upon the size of the pet, as obviously a Great Dane would need something slightly larger than a cushion for a Persian kitten!), stitch together and fill with dried beans to make a bean bag, or polystyrene pieces. Embroider the animal's name onto the cushion, and you have a really personal gift for any pet-lover.

Glove Puppets
Young children love glove puppets, and a little family of them would soon become cherished friends. For the basic shape of the puppet, cut out two pieces as with the doll, and stitch around the outside, leaving the bottom part open. Turn the glove inside out and then decorate with fabric and wool. Do bear in mind the size of the child's hand. A puppet that fits you is going to swamp a four-year-old's hand. If you have some odd socks, these can be used up making glove puppets. Two button eyes and a felt tongue can quickly produce a very realistic snake:

Alternatively a pair of ordinary mittens can be given a felt face, perhaps one happy and one sad.

Miniature Garden
A pot plant makes a nice present, but for something a little more personal and unusual, why not take an attractive pot and put in a variety of different plants to make an interesting display? A couple of different ivies, some asparagus fern, a coloured cactus and so on can soon build up a beautiful miniature garden. Alternatively a little herb garden in a tray, or a pot filled with hyacinth or daffodil bulbs that will bloom after Christmas could be prepared. Ideal for someone with no garden to brighten up the dull winter days.

Christmas Candles
Visit a craft shop and you will find all the equipment necessary for making your own candles. Once you have the basic materials, you will find candlemaking a very relaxing and rewarding hobby. To

make them you need some candle wick, which is sold in reels or on cards, some candle wax, which is sold in granule form, and a substance called stearin which makes the candles set firm and rock hard. Candles do actually improve with keeping because they become harder. To make candles all you need is an old saucepan in which you put nine parts of wax and one part of stearin. Heat the two gently together, and your mixture is ready. If allowed to cool, it becomes malleable and can be moulded with the hands into various shapes. Old cream cartons make excellent moulds. Tie the wick to a pencil and suspend it over the centre of the pot so that, when the wax has set around it, the wick will go right through the centre of the candle:

Buy different coloured waxes and make candles in layers of varying colours, or swirl two coloured waxes together to give a marbled effect. Allow wax to cool slightly (but not set) and pour into wine glasses to make very attractive and unusual candles. For a Christmas candle, make a snowball – use white wax (you can melt down old white candles); roll it into a ball, then roll the ball in silver glitter and you have a sparkling snowball. Don't forget to mould the wax around a wick first, though, otherwise you'll have a candle that will never light!

Countryside Collage
During the autumn gather together as many fine, delicate leaves, flowers and ferns as possible. Press them and dry them under a pile of heavy books between sheets of tissue. Use them to make up an attractive collage picture by gluing them carefully onto a board covered with a piece of card or fabric; a neutral-coloured woven fabric or hessian is perfect. When it is completed, put it in an attractive picture frame under glass.

Waste Paper Bin

As a base take an old tin or a large plastic flower-pot, or buy a cheap plastic bin. Make sure that the inside is perfectly clean, and if necessary cover it with plain white sticky-back plastic. For the outside of the receptacle, which is the most important part, make a discreet study of the person's home that is going to receive your gift and make a mental note of the colour schemes and fabrics used. Decide where you think a bin would be useful, be it in the bathroom for old razor blades and empty toothpaste tubes, in a bedroom for tissues and laddered tights, or in a study for filing letters from the Inland Revenue, and choose a colour and material that would be appropriate – pink velvet for a bedroom, white towelling for a bathroom, hessian wallpaper for a study – and cover the bin neatly with the material, gluing it down firmly. For a neater finish, put a trim of contrasting braid around the top edge. On giving the present you can say specifically, 'This is to go in Roderick's study between the elephant's foot coffee table and the imitation melamine bookshelves,' then, whether they like your present or not, they *won't dare* not use it and your efforts will not have been in vain. The chances are that they will like it and that your personally constructed gift will be used and appreciated.

Paperweight

When you are out walking along a rocky beach, through mountains or valleys, keep your eyes open for unusually shaped and coloured pieces of rock and stone – a lump of pure white quartz, a shattered piece of granite, a time-worn wedge of coloured slate. When you get it home, clean it up, decide which angle looks best, and on the base glue a square of green felt with extra strong glue. If you want to, you can embellish the stone with a subtle and tasteful ornament, a small figure of a stag, a bronze initial, but if you choose an interesting stone, it will stand on its own. If you can say that the stone actually came from the banks of Loch Ness, the top of Snowdon or the foot of Everest, your gift will be given even more significance and value.

Sing Choirs of
Angels

Like so many Christmas traditions, carol singing is one that the Victorians gave a new lease of life to. Although many of the carols that we sing can be traced back to medieval times, apart from a collection published in 1521 few others appeared in print until the mid-nineteenth century. We associate carols solely with Christmas, but the word actually means 'ring dance' and they were originally religious hymns sung at any Christian festival, such as Easter and Whitsun.

Carols have been handed down literally by word of mouth for generations. One of the oldest is the 'Boar's Head Carol', which is still sung each year at Queen's College, Oxford, when a boar's head is carried in for Christmas dinner. The carol appears in that first medieval carol book, half in English and half in Latin. Many of our favourites, however, were written by the Victorians, and it comes as a surprise to many to discover that old favourites like 'Good King Wenceslas' were actually only composed towards the second half of the nineteenth century, although the tunes (as with 'Wenceslas') have a much longer history.

It was the Victorians who started the tradition of 'carol singers' going round to houses to give renderings of much-loved carols. St Thomas' Eve (21 December) is the night on which you should traditionally begin singing carols, although now we hear them played from early December onwards, and why not?

Many ceremonies and carol services take place in the United Kingdom every year, but one of the nicest must surely be the Christingle service held annually in Norwich Cathedral. At the service over five hundred children bear Christingles whilst carols are sung. A Christingle is easy to make. A candle is pushed into the middle of an orange which has been decorated with tiny nuts and almonds, and a ribbon is tied around the orange. The lighted Christingle represents the 'Light of the World', for the orange is symbolic of the world and its people, and the red ribbon symbolizes the blood of Christ. A magic moment in the service is when the children, as if with one breath, blow the candles out.

One of the most famous carol services is the 'Festival of the Nine Lessons and Carols' which is held in King's College Chapel, Cambridge, and is broadcast every year on radio. The first broadcast was in 1930, and it still conveys as much of the true spirit of Christmas as it ever has. The service always begins with 'Once in Royal David's City', sung by a boy soprano; nine carols are sung in all, and nine lessons are read by nine different readers, telling the whole of the Christmas story.

In many parts of the country the 'visit of the Waits' was strongly associated with carol singing. The 'Waits' were a group of musicians who travelled around the towns and villages playing Christmas carols and popular tunes during the week preceding Christmas. The tunes were probably made all the more merry by the fact that the Waits were usually invited by the various householders to join them in a drink of mulled wine after their performance, and generally joined them in singing carols. In the nineteenth century Waits were joined by singers carrying lanterns, and often collected money for the poor.

Today carol singing is one of the chief joys of the festive season. Carols are generally divided into four kinds: the religious hymn-like carol, such as 'It Came Upon the Midnight Clear', the words of which were written in 1849 by E.H. Sears and the tune composed by Sir Arthur Sullivan; the non-religious carol, like 'Good King Wenceslas'; the soft lullaby-like carols that children love so much, especially 'Away in a Manger', which is called 'Luther's Cradle Hymn' and associated with Martin Luther, although it is not thought that he wrote it; and the lively, bright carols, such as 'Ding Dong Merrily on High' and 'Deck the Halls', a Welsh carol that is of Druid origin. Many pagan tunes were handed on to the Christian Church and have now become firm favourites.

So that you can continue the musical traditions of Christmas, here are the words and music to some of the most popular and best-loved carols. Gather with your family around the piano, tune up the guitar or dust off your old tin whistle and bring a little Christmas harmony to your home. Don't worry if you're not a singer: musical instruments in the Middle Ages had a very small range of notes and, as many carol tunes are from that period of history, they are easy to sing!

God Rest You Merry, Gentlemen

God rest you merry, gentlemen,
Let nothing you dismay,
For Jesus Christ our Saviour
Was born upon this day,
To save us all from Satan's power
When we were gone astray.

O tidings of comfort and joy, comfort and joy
O tidings of comfort and joy.

In Bethlehem in Jewry
This blessed babe was born,
And laid within a manger,
Upon this blessed morn;
The which his mother Mary
Nothing did take in scorn:

O tidings of comfort and joy ...

From God our heavenly Father
A blessed Angel came,
And unto certain shepherds
Brought tidings of the same,
How that in Bethlehem was born
The Son of God by name:

O tidings of comfort and joy ...

'Fear not', then said the angel,
'Let nothing you afright,
This day is born a Saviour,
Of virtue, power and might;
So frequently to vanquish all
The friends of Satan quite':

O tidings of comfort and joy ...

The shepherds at those tidings
Rejoicèd much in mind,
And left their flocks a-feeding,
In tempest, storm and wind,
And went to Bethlehem straightaway
This blessèd babe to find:

O tidings of comfort and joy ...

But when to Bethlehem they came,
Whereat this infant lay,
They found him in a manger,
Where oxen feed on hay;
His mother Mary kneeling,
Unto the Lord did pray:

O tidings of comfort and joy ...

Now to the Lord sing praises,
All you within this place,
And with true love and brotherhood
Each other now embrace;
This holy tide of Christmas
All others doth deface:

O tidings of comfort and joy ...

O Come, All Ye Faithful

O come, all ye faithful,
Joyful and triumphant,
O come ye, O come ye to Bethlehem;
Come and behold Him,
Born the King of angels;

O come, let us adore Him,
O come, let us adore Him,
O come, let us adore Him, Christ the Lord

Sing, choirs of angels
Sing in exultation
Sing, all ye citizens of heaven above,
Glory to God
In the highest:

O come, let us adore Him ...

Yea, Lord, we greet Thee,
Born this happy morning;
Jesus, to Thee be glory given,
Word of the Father,
Now in flesh appearing:

O come, let us adore Him ...

While Shepherds Watched Their Flocks

While shepherds watched their flocks by night,
All seated on the ground,
The angel of the Lord came down,
And glory shone around.
'Fear not,' said he (for mighty dread
Had seized their troubled mind);
'Glad tidings of great joy I bring
To you, and all mankind.

'To you in David's town this day
Is born of David's line
A saviour, who is Christ the Lord;

And this shall be the sign:
The heavenly babe you there shall find
To human view displayed,
All meanly wrapped in swathing bands,
And in a manger laid.'

Thus spake the seraph: and forthwith
Appeared a shining throng
Of angels praising God, who thus
Addressed their joyful song:
'All glory be to God on high,
And to the earth be peace;
Good-will henceforth from heaven to men
Begin, and never cease.'

The First Noel

The first Noel the angel did say
Was to certain poor shepherds in fields as they lay;
In fields where they lay keeping their sheep
On a cold winter's night that was so deep.

Noel, Noel, Noel, Noel,
Born is the King of Israel.

They lookèd up and saw a star,
Shining in the East beyond them far,
And to the earth it gave great light,
And so it continued both day and night.

Noel, Noel ...

And by the light of that same star,
Three wise men came from country far;
To seek for a King was their intent,
And to follow the star wherever it went.

Noel, Noel ...

This star drew nigh to the north-west,
O'er Bethlehem it took its rest,
And there it did stop and stay,
Right over the place where Jesus lay.

Noel, Noel ...

Then entered in those wise men three
Fell reverently upon their knee,
And offered there, in His presence,
Their gold, and myrrh, and frankincense.

Noel, Noel ...

Then let us all with one accord
Sing praises to our heavenly Lord,
That hath made heaven and earth of nought,
And with His blood mankind hath bought.

Noel, Noel ...

Deck the Halls

Deck the halls with boughs of holly,
Fa la la la la la la la la.
'Tis the season to be jolly.
Fa la la la la la la la la.
Don we now our gay apparel,
Fa la la la la la la la la.
Troll the ancient Yuletide carol,
Fa la la la la la la la la.

See the blazing Yule before us,
Fa la la la la la la la la.
Strike the harp and join the chorus,
Fa la la la la la la la la.
Follow me in merry measure,
Fa la la la la la la la la.
While I tell of Yuletide treasure,
Fa la la la la la la la la.

Fast away the old year passes,
Fa la la la la la la la la.
Fail the new ye lads and lasses,
Fa la la la la la la la la.
Sing we joyous altogether,
Fa la la la la la la la la.
Heedless of the wind and weather,
Fa la la la la la la la la.

Hark! The Herald Angels Sing

Hark! the herald angels sing,
Glory to the new-born King,
Peace on earth and mercy mild,
God and sinners reconciled!'
Joyful, all ye nations, rise,
Join the triumph of the skies;
With th'angelic host proclaim,
'Christ is born in Bethlehem!'
  Hark! the herald angels sing,
  Glory to the new-born King.'

Christ, by highest heaven adored,
Christ, the everlasting Lord,

Late in time behold Him come
Offspring of the Virgin's womb;
Veiled in flesh the Godhead see;
Hail the incarnate Deity!
Pleased as man with man to dwell,
Jesus, our Emmanuel:

Hail the heaven-born Prince of Peace!
Hail the Sun of Righteousness!
Light and life to all He brings,
Risen with healing in His wings
Mild He lays His glory by,
Born that man no more may die,
Born to raise the sons of earth,
Born to give them second birth.

The Holly and the Ivy

The holly and the ivy,
When they are both full grown,
Of all the trees that are in the wood,
The holly bears the crown:

The rising of the sun
And the running of the deer,
The playing of the merry organ,
Sweet singing in the choir.

The holly bears a blossom,
As white as the lily flower,
And Mary bore sweet Jesus Christ,
To be our sweet Saviour:

The rising of the sun ...

The holly bears a berry,
As red as any blood,
And Mary bore sweet Jesus Christ,
To do poor sinners good:

The rising of the sun ...

The holly bears a prickle,
As sharp as any thorn,
And Mary bore sweet Jesus Christ
On Christmas day in the morn:

The rising of the sun ...

The holly bears a bark,
As bitter as any gall,
And Mary bore sweet Jesus Christ
For to redeem us all:

The rising of the sun ...

Angels from the Realms of Glory

Angels from the realms of glory,
Wing your flight o'er all the earth;
Ye who sang creation's story
Now proclaim Messiah's birth:

Gloria in excelsis Deo.
Gloria in excelsis Deo.

Shepherds in the field abiding,
Watching o'er your flocks by night,
God with man is now residing;
Yonder shines the infant Light:

Gloria ...

Sages, leave your contemplations;
Brighter visions beam afar;
Seek the great Desire of Nations;
Ye have seen his natal star:

Gloria ...

Saints, before the altar bending,
Watching long in hope and fear,
Suddenly the Lord, descending,
In His temple shall appear:

Gloria ...

Though an infant now we view him,
He shall fill his father's throne,
Gather all the nations to him;
Every knee shall then bow down:

Gloria ...

We Wish You a Merry Christmas

We wish you a merry Christmas,
We wish you a merry Christmas,
We wish you a merry Christmas and a happy New Year.

Chorus
Good tidings we bring to you and your king.
We wish you a merry Christmas and a happy New Year.

We all want some figgy pudding,
We all want some figgy pudding,
We all want some figgy pudding, so bring some out here!

Chorus

We won't go until we get some,
We won't go until we get some,
We won't go until we get some, so bring some out here!

Chorus

We wish you a merry Christmas,
We wish you a merry Christmas,
We wish you a merry Christmas, and a happy New Year.

Away in a Manger

Away in a manger, no crib for a bed
The little Lord Jesus laid down His sweet head.
The stars in the bright sky looked down where He lay,
The little Lord Jesus asleep on the hay.

The cattle are lowing, the Baby awakes,
But little Lord Jesus no crying he makes.
I love thee, Lord Jesus! Look down from the sky,
And stay by my side until morning is nigh.

Be near me, Lord Jesus; I ask Thee to stay
Close by me for ever, and love me, I pray.
Bless all the dear children in Thy tender care,
And fit us for Heaven, to live with Thee there.

The Birds

From out of a wood did a cuckoo fly,
   Cuckoo,
He came to a manger with joyful cry,
   Cuckoo,
He hopped, he curtsied, round he flew,
   Cuckoo, cuckoo, cuckoo.

A pigeon flew over to Galilee,
   Vrercroo,
He strutted and cooed, and was full of glee,
   Vrercroo,
And showed with jewelled wings unfurled,
His joy that Christ was in the world,
   Vrercroo, vrercroo, vrercroo.

A dove settled down upon Nazareth,
   Tsucroo,
And tenderly chanted with all his breath,
   Tsucroo,
'O you,' he cooed, 'so good and true,
My beauty do I give to you –
   Tsucroo, tsucroo, tsucroo.'

It Came Upon the Midnight Clear

It came upon the midnight clear,
That glorious song of old,
From angels bending near the earth
To touch their harps of gold.
'Peace on the earth, good will to men,
From heav'n's all gracious King.'
The world in solemn stillness lay
To hear the angels sing.

Still through the cloven skies they come,
With peaceful wings unfurled,
And still their heavenly music floats
O'er all the weary world:
Above its sad and lowly pains
They bend on hovering wing,
And ever o'er its Babel sounds
The blessed angels sing.

For lo! the days are hastening on,
By prophet bards foretold,
When with the ever-circling years
Comes round the age of gold;
When peace shall over all the earth
Its ancient splendours fling,
And the whole world send back the song
Which now the angels sing.

Silent Night, Holy Night

Silent night, holy night!
All is calm, all is bright,
Round yon Virgin Mother and Child!
Holy Infant so tender and mild,
Sleep in heavenly peace,
Sleep in heavenly peace.

Silent night, holy night!
Shepherds first saw the light,
Heard resounding clear and long
Far and near the angel song;
Christ the Saviour is here,
Christ the Saviour is here.

Silent night, holy night!
Son of God, oh how bright
Love is smiling from Thy face
Peals for us the hour of grace:
Christ our Saviour is born,
Christ our Saviour is born.

Here We Come A-Wassailing

Here we come a-wassailing, among the leaves so green,
Here we come a-wandering, so fair to be seen.
Love and joy come to you, and to you your wassail too,
And God bless you, and send you a happy New Year,
And God send you a happy New Year.

We are not daily beggars, that beg from door to door,
But we are neighbours' children whom you have seen before.

Chorus

We have got a little purse of stretching leather skin;
We want a little money to line it well within.

Chorus

God bless the master of this house, likewise the mistress too;
And all the little children that round the table go.

Chorus

The Coventry Carol

Herod the king in his raging
Charged he hath this day
His men of might in his own sight,
All children young to slay.

Then woe is me, poor Child, for Thee!
And ever, morn and day,
For Thy parting nor say nor sing
Bye, bye, lullay, lullay.

Lullay, Thou little tiny child,
Bye, bye, lullay, lullay,
Lullay, Thou little tiny child,
Bye, bye, lullay, lullay.

Oh sisters, too, how may we do?
For to preserve this day,
This poor Youngling, for whom we sing
Bye, bye, lullay, lullay.

Mid-Winter

In the bleak mid-winter
Frosty wind made moan,
Earth stood hard as iron,
Water like a stone;
Snow had fallen, snow on snow,
Snow on snow,
In the bleak mid-winter,
Long ago.

Our God, heav'n cannot hold him
Nor earth sustain;
Heav'n and earth shall flee away
When he comes to reign:
In the bleak mid-winter
A stable-place sufficed
The Lord God Almighty
Jesus Christ.

Enough for him, whom cherubim
Worship night and day,
A breastful of milk,
And a mangerful of hay;
Enough for him, Whom angels
Fall down before,
The ox and ass and camel
Which adore.

Angels and Archangels
May have gathered there,
Cherubim and Seraphim
Thronged the air:
But only his mother
In her maiden bliss
Worshipped the Beloved
With a kiss.

What can I give him,
Poor as I am?
If I were a shepherd
I would bring a lamb;
If I were a wise man
I would do my part;
Yet what can I give him –
Give my heart.

Good King Wenceslas

Good King Wenceslas look'd out,
On the Feast of Stephen,*
When the snow lay round about,
Deep and crisp and even;
Brightly shone the moon that night,
Though the frost was cruel,
When a poor man came in sight,
Gath'ring winter fuel.

'Hither, page, and stand by me,
If thou know'st it, telling.
Yonder peasant, who is he?
Where and what his dwelling?'
'Sire, he lives a good league hence,
Underneath the mountain,
Right against the forest fence,
By Saint Agnes' fountain.'

   * Well, no actually, he didn't. Wenceslas *did* exist – he was a tenth-century
Bohemian prince, saint and martyr – but this story is a figment of the Victorian
imagination of John Neale who wrote the carol.

'Bring me flesh, and bring me wine,
Bring me pine logs hither:
Thou and I wilt see him dine,
When we bear them thither.'
Page and monarch, forth they went,
Forth they went together;
Through the rude wind's wild lament,
And the bitter weather.

'Sire, the night is darker now,
And the wind blows stronger;
Fails my heart, I know not how;
I can go no longer.'
'Mark my footsteps, my good page;
Tread thou in them boldly:
Thou shalt find the winter's rage
Freeze thy blood less coldly.'

In his master's steps he trod,
Where the snow lay dinted;
Heat was in the very sod
Which the saint had printed.
Therefore, Christian men, be sure,
Wealth or rank possessing,
Ye who now will bless the poor,
Shall yourselves find blessing.

ALL IS CALM

ALL IS BRIGHT

'Twas the night before Christmas ... or maybe it was two days *after* Christmas; whenever it was, our forefathers who really knew the art of capturing the Christmas spirit entirely would sit down by the fireside in quiet contemplation and read traditional poetry and stories of a seasonal nature. In the nineteenth century, the heyday of the British Christmas, readings were an essential part of Christmas entertainment.

At the tail end of the twentieth century, we have drifted away from the idea of home entertainments. Today Christmas is delivered in commercial packages and is transmitted by satellite. Whilst grandma is glued to the video, the kids play with their mini-computers. On Christmas Day in the British Isles the average family watches nine hours of television. Small wonder that the olde worlde charms of traditional Christmases have been lost!

As Christmas is a time of traditions, it is often fun to try to recapture the spirit of an age gone by. One way of doing this is to revive the seasonal tradition of our Victorian great-great-grandfathers, who really did gather the whole family around the fireside and read aloud to them. Tear-jerking ballads like 'Billy's Rose', chilling tales of ghosts and spooks such as the stories of Bret Harte, old Dickensian classics that are firm favourites with young and old alike, sentimental poetry, nostalgic rhymes and melodramatic pieces that stir the blood and warm the heart, if read aloud with feeling, have the power to beat any television programme.

Bring back this sadly lapsed tradition by entertaining your family with some Christmas renditions. A Victorian book on the art of recitation provides some helpful hints to anyone wishing to read aloud:

> ... Remember that you are about to paint a picture in words. To do this effectively, avoid daubing in lurid colours. Regard your mind as a palette, your voice as the brush, and colour tones are sympathy, tranquillity, gentleness, optimism, faithfulness and clearness of expression.

The following simple rules will prove of great assistance:

1.   Breathe easily, inflating the lungs slowly, and without effort or sound.

2.   Speak clearly and distinctly, and avoid shouting.

3.   Sound the consonants, but do not hiss them.

4. Sound the syllables distinctly, but without undue emphasis.
5. Sound the definite article without giving it too much importance.
6. Read brightly and naturally.
7. Avoid monotony; graduate tones by feeling.
8. Understand clearly and sympathetically what is studied.
9. Read with earnestness, but without heaviness.
10. Mind pauses and emphasis.

Stirring stuff indeed! Almost as dramatic as the readings themselves, yet it is sound advice that still holds good today.

In the pages that follow, a selection of literature for Christmas is presented – a special collection of stories, poems and fragments of great classics that bring a special warmth to the heart of the reader at Christmas. There are old favourites here – 'The Night Before Christmas' and 'Christmas Day in the Workhouse' – but some may be totally unfamiliar to you. They are certain to become firm favourites, whether rendered aloud in the old tradition or simply read quietly to yourself as you relax beside the fire at the end of a hectic day.

To begin, no Christmas could possibly be complete without an extract from the very first Christmas story ...

FOR UNTO US A CHILD IS BORN ...

And it came to pass in those days, that there went out a decree from Caesar Augustus, that all the world should be taxed. (And this taxing was first made when Cyrenius was governor of Syria.) And all went out to be taxed, everyone into his own city. And Joseph also went up from Galilee, out of the city of Nazareth, into Judea, unto the city of David, which is called Bethlehem, (because he was of the house and lineage of David,) to be taxed with Mary his espoused wife, being great with child. And so it was, that, while they were there, the days were accomplished that she should be delivered. And she brought forth her firstborn son, and wrapped him in swaddling clothes, and laid him in a manger; because there was no room for them in the inn.

And there were in the same country shepherds abiding in the field, keeping watch over their flock by night. And, lo, the angel of the Lord came upon them, and the glory of the Lord shone round about them; and they were sore afraid. And the angel said unto them, Fear not: for, behold, I bring you good tidings of great joy, which shall be to all people. For unto you is born this day in the city of David a Saviour, which is Christ the Lord. And this shall be a sign unto you; Ye shall find the babe wrapped in swaddling clothes, lying in a manger. And suddenly there was with the angel a multitude of the heavenly host praising God, and saying, Glory to God in the highest, and on earth peace, good will toward men.

And it came to pass, as the angels were gone away from them into heaven, the Shepherds said one to another, Let us now go even unto Bethlehem, and see this thing which has come to pass, which the Lord hath made known to us. And they came with haste, and found Mary and Joseph, and the babe lying in a manger. And when they had seen it, they made known abroad the saying which was told them concerning the child. And all they that heard it wondered at those things which were told them by the shepherds. But Mary kept all these things, and pondered them in her heart. And the shepherds returned, glorifying and praising God for all the things that they had heard and seen, as it was told unto them.

Now when Jesus was born in Bethlehem of Judea in the days of Herod the king, behold, there came wise men from the East to Jerusalem, saying, Where is he that is born King of the Jews? for we have seen his star in the east, and are come to worship him. When Herod the king had heard these things, he was troubled, and all Jerusalem with him. And when he had gathered all the chief priests and scribes of the people together, he demanded of them where Christ should be born. And they said unto him, In Bethlehem of Judea: for thus it is written by the prophet, And thou Bethlehem, in the land of Judah, art not the least among the princes of Judah: for out of thee shall come a Governor, that shall rule my people Israel. Then Herod, when he had privily called the wise men, inquired of them diligently what time the star appeared. And he sent them to Bethlehem, and said, Go and search diligently for the young child; and when ye have found him, bring me word again, that I may come and worship him also.

When they had heard the king, they departed; and, lo, the star which they saw in the east, went before them, till it came and stood over where the young child was. When they saw the star they rejoiced with exceeding great joy. And when they were come into the house, they saw the young child with Mary his mother, and fell down, and worshipped him: and when they had opened their treasures, they presented unto him gifts; gold, and frankincense, and myrrh. And being warned of God in a dream that they should not return to Herod, they departed into their own country another way.

ON THE MORNING OF CHRIST'S NATIVITY

By John Milton

The shepherds on the lawn,
Or ere the point of dawn,
   Sat simply chatting in a rustic row;
Full little thought they than
That the mighty Pan
Was kindly come to live with them below;
Perhaps their loves, or else their sheep,
Was all that did their silly thoughts so busy keep.

When such music sweet
Their hearts and ears did greet,
   As never was by mortal finger strook;
Divinely warbled voice
Answering the stringed noise,
   As all their souls in blissful rapture took:
The air such pleasure loth to lose,
With thousand echoes still prolongs each heav'nly close.

At last surrounds their sight
A globe of circular light,

That with long beams the shame-fac'd night array'd;
The helmed cherabim
And sworded seraphim
    Are seen in glittering ranks with wings display'd,
Harping in loud and solemn quire
With unexpressive notes to Heav'n's new-born heir.

Such music (as 'tis said)
Before was never made,
    But when of old the sons of morning sung;
While the Creator Great
His constellations set,
    And the well-balanc'd world on hinges hung,
And cast the dark foundations deep,
And bid the welt'ring waves their oozy channel keep.

Ring out ye crystal spheres,
Once bless our human ears,
    (If ye have powers to touch our senses so),
And let your silver chime
Move in melodious time;
    And let the base of Heaven's deep organ blow;
And with your nine-fold harmony
Make up full consort to th'angelic symphony.

For if such holy song
Enwrap our fancy long,
    Time will run back, and fetch the age of gold;
And speckl'd Vanity
Will sicken soon and die,
    And leprous Sin will melt from earthly mould;
And Hell itself will pass away,
And leave her dolorous mansions to the peering day.

But see the virgin blest,
Hath laid her babe to rest.
    Time is our tedious song should here have ending:
Heaven's youngest teemed star,
Hath fix'd her polish'd charm
    Her sleeping Lord with handmaid lamp attending.
And all about the courtly stable,
Bright-harness'd angels sit in order serviceable.

THE LOUIS-D'OR:
A FRENCH CHRISTMAS STORY
By François Coppée

When Lucien de Hemm saw his last bill for a hundred francs clawed by the banker's rake, when he rose from the roulette table where he had just lost the debris of his little fortune, scraped together from this supreme battle, he experienced something like vertigo and thought that he should fall. His brain was muddled; his legs were limp and trembling. He threw himself upon the leather lounge that circumscribed the gambling table.

For a few moments he mechanically followed the clandestine proceedings of that hell in which he had sullied the best years of his youth, recognized the worn profiles of the gamblers under the merciless glare of the three great shadeless lamps, listened to the clicking and the sliding of the gold over the felt, realized that he was bankrupt, lost, remembered that in the top drawer of his dressing-table lay a pair of pistols – the very pistols of which General de Hemm, his father, had made noble use at the attack of Zaatcha; then, overcome by exhaustion, he sank into a heavy sleep.

When he awoke, his mouth was clammy and his tongue stuck to his palate. He realized by a glance at the clock that he had scarcely slept a half-hour, and he felt the imperious necessity of going out to get a breath of the fresh night air.

The hands on the dial pointed exactly to a quarter to twelve.

As he rose and stretched his arms it occurred to him that it was Christmas Eve, and by one of those ironical freaks of the memory, he felt as though he was once more a child, ready to stand his little boot on the hearth before going to bed. Just then old Dronski, one of the pillars of the trade, the traditional Pole, wrapped in the greasy, worn cloak adorned with frogs and passementerie, came up to Lucien muttering something behind his dirty, grayish beard.

'Lend me five francs, will you, Monsieur? I haven't stirred from this place for two days, and for two whole days seventeen hasn't come out once. You may laugh at me all you like, but I'll bet you my fist that when the clock strikes twelve, seventeen will be the winning number.'

Lucien de Hemm shrugged his shoulders; and fumbling through his pockets, he found that he had not even money enough to comply with that feature of gambling etiquette known among the frequenters of the establishment as 'the Pole's hundred cents'.

How could he give what he did not have? And if he had found but a single louis, would he not hazard it to retrieve the fortune he had lost?

He passed into the ante-chamber, put on his hat and cloak, and disappeared down the narrow stairway with the agility of people who have a fever. During the four hours which Lucien had spent in the den it had snowed heavily, and the street, one of those narrow wedges between two rows of high buildings in the very heart of Paris, was intensely white.

Above, in the calm sky, cold stars glittered.

The exhausted gambler shivered under his furs, and hurried along with a blank despair in his heart, thinking of the pistols that awaited him in the top drawer of his dressing-table. He had not gone a hundred feet when he stopped suddenly before a heart-rending spectacle, one that would have touched the sympathies of all but the most hardened gamblers.

On a stone bench, near the monumental doorway of a wealthy residence, sat a little girl, six or seven years old, barely covered by a ragged black gown. She had fallen asleep there in spite of the bitter cold, her body bent forward in a pitiful posture of resigned exhaustion. Her poor little head and her dainty shoulders had moulded themselves into the angle of the freezing wall.

One of her worn slippers had fallen from her dangling foot and lay in the snow before her. Lucien de Hemm mechanically thrust his hand into his vest pocket, but he remembered that he had not even been able to fee the club waiter.

He went up to the child, however, impelled by an instinct of pity.

He meant, no doubt, to pick her up and take her home with him, to give her shelter for the night, when suddenly he saw something glitter in the little slipper at his feet.

He stopped. It was a louis-d'or.

Some charitable soul had passed there, and at the pathetic sight of the little shoe in the snow, had remembered the poetic Christmas legend, and with discreet fingers had dropped a splendid gift, so that the forsaken little one might still believe in the presents of the Child-Christ, and might wake with renewed faith in the midst of her misery.

A gold louis!

That meant many days of rest and comfort for the little beggar.

Lucien was just about to waken her and surprise her with her good fortune, when, in a strange hallucination, he heard a voice in his ear, which whispered with the drawling inflection of the old Pole:

'I haven't stirred from this place for two days, and for two whole days seventeen hasn't come out once. I'll bet you my fist that when the clock strikes twelve, seventeen will be the winning number.'

Then this youth, who was twenty-three years of age, the descendant of a race of honest men – this youth, who bore a great military name, and had never been guilty of an unmanly act – conceived a monstrous thought; an insane desire took possession of him.

He looked anxiously up and down the street, and having assured himself that he had no witness, he knelt, and reaching out cautiously with trembling fingers, stole the treasure from the little shoe, then rose with a spring and ran breathlessly down the street.

He rushed like a madman up the stairs of the gambling-house, flung open the door with his fist, and burst into the room at the first stroke of midnight. He threw the gold piece on the table and cried:

'Seventeen!''

Seventeen won.

He then pushed the whole pile on the 'red'. The red won.

He placed thirty-six louis on the red.

By some kindly touch of fairy chance the red came up a winner.

He now won seventy-two louis.

The crowd pressed closer to the table and peered anxiously over each other's shoulders as the play grew more and more exciting.

He left the seventy-two louis on the same colour. The red came out again.

He doubled the stakes twice, three times, and always with the same success.

Before him was a huge pile of gold and bank-notes. He tried the 'twelve', the 'column' – he worked every combination. His luck was something unheard of, something almost supernatural. One might have believed the ivory ball, in its frenzied dance around the table, had been bewitched, magnetized by this feverish gambler, and obeyed his will.

Those who had been losing all evening, and, though with all their money spent, still hovered around the gaming-table, fascinated by the mere association, looked with envy on the daring man who seemed to hold Fortune a slave. With a few bold strokes he had won back the bundle of bank-notes he had lost in the early part of the evening. Then he staked two and three hundred louis at a time, and as his fantastic luck never failed him, he soon won back the whole capital that had constituted his inherited fortune.

Old Dronski the Pole, who had asked only for a beggarly five francs but a half-hour before, glared at Lucien as if he could devour him; all this money he (Dronski) might have had. Was it not his by right? Was not the tip to play 'seventeen' at midnight his? And he had missed it all, this fortune, for a mere pittance!

In his haste to begin the game Lucien had not even thought of taking off his fur-lined coat, the great pockets of which were now swollen with the rolls of bank-notes and heavy with the weight of gold.

And still Lucien played on. His face was flushed, his hand unsteady, and a reckless, vibrant bravado crept into his voice. Not knowing where to put the money that was steadily accumulating before him, he stuffed it away in the inside and outside pockets of his coat, his vest, his trousers, in his cigar-case, his handkerchief. Everything became a recipient.

And still he played on, and still he won, his brain whirling the meantime like that of a madman or a drunkard. It was amazing to see him standing there throwing gold on the table by the handful with that haughty gesture of absolute certainty and disdain. But withal there was a gnawing at his heart, something that felt like a red-hot iron there, and he could not rid himself of the vision of the child in the snow – the child whom he had robbed.

'In just a few minutes,' he thought, 'I will go back to her. She must be there in the same place. Of course she must be there. It is no crime, after all. I will make it right to her – it will be no crime. Quite the contrary. I will leave here in a few moments when the clock strikes again. I swear it. Just as soon as the clock strikes again I will stop; I will go straight to where she is; I will take her up in my arms and will carry her home with me asleep. I have done her no harm; I have made a fortune for her. I will keep her with me and educate her; I will love her as I would love a child of my own, and I will take care of her always – for as long as she lives.'

But the clock struck one, a quarter past, half-past, and Lucien was still there. Finally, a few minutes before two, the man opposite him rose brusquely and said in a loud voice:

'The bank is broken, gentlemen; this will do for tonight.'

Lucien started, and wedging his way brutally through the gamblers, who pressed around him in envious admiration, hurried out into the street and ran as fast as he could toward the stone bench. In a moment he saw by the light of the gas that the child was still there.

'God be praised!' he cried, and his heart gave a throb for joy. Yes, here she was! He took her little hand in his. Poor little hand, how cold it was! He caught her under the arms and lifted her. Her head fell back, but she did not awake.

'The happy sleep of childhood,' he thought.

A motley crowd of revellers from some masquerade passed by on the other side, shouting with merry peals of laughter and badinage; yet he scarcely noticed them, scarcely heard them, so intent was he on the chilled little bundle of humanity in his arms.

He pressed her close to his breast to warm her, and with a vague presentiment he tried to arouse her from this heavy sleep by kissing her eyelids. But he realized then with horror that through the child's half-open lids her eyes were dull, glassy, fixed. A distracting suspicion flashed through his mind. He put his lips to the child's mouth; he felt no breath.

'*Mon Dieu! Mon Dieu!* What have I done?' he cried in his despair. It was murder, a life taken for a paltry louis. What could he do now?

While Lucien had been building a fortune with the louis stolen from this little one, she, homeless, forsaken, had perished with the cold. Lucien felt a suffocating knot at his throat. In his anguish he tried to cry out; and in the effort which he made he awoke from his nightmare, and found himself on the leather lounge in the gambling-room where he had fallen asleep a little before midnight. The *garçon* of the den had gone home at about five o'clock, and out of pity had not wakened him.

A misty December dawn made the window-panes pale. Lucien went out, pawned his watch, took a bath, then went over to the

Bureau of Recruits and enlisted as a volunteer in the First
Regiment of the Chasseurs d'Afrique.

Lucien de Hemm is now a lieutenant. He has not a cent in the
world but his pay. He manages to make that do, however, for he is
a steady officer and never touches a card.

He even contrives to economize, it would seem; for a few days
ago a comrade, who was following him up one of the steep streets
of the Kasba, saw him stop and lay a piece of money in the lap of a
little Spanish girl who had fallen asleep in a doorway.

His comrade was startled at the poor lieutenant's generosity, for
this piece of money was a gold louis.

BILLY'S ROSE

By George R. Simms

Billy's dead and gone to glory – so is Billy's sister Nell:
There's a tale I know about them, were I poet I would tell;
Soft it comes, with perfume laden, like a breath of country air,
Wafted down the filthy alley, spreading fragrant odours there.

In that vile and filthy alley, long ago, one winter's day,
Dying quick of want and fever, hapless, patient, Billy lay;
While beside him sat his sister, in the garret's dismal gloom,
Cheering with her gentle presence, Billy's pathway to the tomb.

Many a tale of elf and fairy did she tell the dying child,
Till his eyes half lost their anguish, and his worn, wan features
    smiled:
Tales herself had heard haphazard, caught amid the Babel roar,
Lisped about by tiny gossips, play round their mother's door.

Then she felt his wasted fingers tighten feebly as she told
How beyond this dismal alley lay a land of shining gold,
Where, when all the pain was over – where, when all the tears
    were shed –
He would be a white-frocked angel, with a gold thing on his
    head.

Then she told some garbled story of a kind-eyed Saviour's love,
How he'd built for little children great big playgrounds up
above,
Where they sang and played at hop-scotch and at horses all the
day,
And where beadles and policemen never frighten them away.

This was Nell's idea of Heaven – just a bit of what she'd heard,
With a little bit invented and a little bit inferred;
But her brother lay and listened, and he seemed to understand,
For he closed his eyes and murmured he could see the Promised
land.

'Yes,' he whispered, 'I can see it – I can see it, sister Nell;
Oh, the children look so happy, and they're all so strong and
well;
I can see them there with Jesus – He is playing with them too!
Let us run away and join them, if there's room for me and you.'

She was eight, this little maiden, and her life had all been spent
In the garret and the alley, where they starved to pay the rent;
Where a drunken father's curses and a drunken mother's blows
Drove her forth into the gutter from the day's dawn to its close.

But she knew enough, this outcast, just to tell the sinking boy,
'You must die before you're able all these blessings to enjoy.
You must die,' she whisperd, 'Billy, and I'm not even ill;
But I'll come to you, dear brother, – yes, I promise that I will.

'You are dying, little brother, – you are dying, oh, so fast;
I heard father say to mother that he knew you couldn't last.
They'll put you in a coffin, then you'll wake up and be there,
While I'm left alone to suffer in this garret bleak and bare.'

'Yes, I know it,' answered Billy, 'Ah, but sister, I don't mind,
Gentle Jesus will not beat me; He's not cruel or unkind.
But I can't help thinking, Nelly, I should like to take away
Something, sister, that you gave me, I might look at every day.

'In the summer you remember how the Mission took us out

157

To a great green lovely meadow, where we played and ran about,
And the van that took us halted by a sweet, bright patch of land,
Where the fine red blossoms grow, dear, half as big as mother's hand.

'Nell, I asked the good kind teacher what they called such flowers as those,
And he told me, I remember, that their pretty name was rose.
I have never seen them since, dear – how I wish that I had one!
Just to keep and think of you, Nell, when I'm up beyond the sun.'

Not a word said little Nelly; but at night, when Billy slept,
On she flung her scanty garments, and then down the stairs she crept.
Through the silent streets of London she ran nimbly as a fawn,
Running on and running ever till the night had changed to dawn.

When the foggy sun had risen, and the mist had cleared away
All around her, wrapped in snowdrift, there the open country lay.
She was tired, her limbs were frozen, and the roads had cut her feet,
But there came no flowery gardens her poor tearful eyes to greet.

She had traced the road by asking – she had learnt the way to go;
She had found the famous meadow – it was wrapped in cruel snow;
Not a buttercup or daisy, not a single verdant blade
Showed its head above its prison. Then she knelt her down and prayed.

With her eyes upcast to Heaven, down she sank upon the ground,
And she prayed to God to tell her where the roses might be found.
Then the cold blast numbed her senses, and her sight grew

strangely dim;
And a sudden, awful tremor seemed to seize her every limb.

'Oh, a rose!' she moaned, 'good Jesus, just a rose to take to Bill!'
And as she prayed a chariot came thundering down the hill;
And a lady sat there, toying with a red rose, rare and sweet;
As she passed she flung it from her, it fell at Nelly's feet.

Just a word her lord had spoken caused her ladyship to fret,
And the rose had been his present, so she flung it in a pet;
But the poor, half-blinded Nelly thought it fallen from the
skies,
And she murmured, 'Thank you, Jesus!' as she clasped the
dainty prize.

Lo! that night from out the alley did a child's soul pass away,
From dirt and sin and misery to where God's children play.
Lo! that night a wild, fierce snowstorm burst in fury o'er the
land,
And that morn they found Nell frozen, with the red rose in her
hand.

Billy's dead, and gone to glory – so is Billy's sister Nell,
Am I bold to say this happened in the land where angels dwell –
That the children met in Heaven, after all their earthly woes,
And that Nelly kissed her brother, and said 'Billy, here's your
Rose'?

SCROOGE'S CHRISTMAS

By Charles Dickens: *A Christmas Carol*

Before

Once upon a time – of all the good days in the year, on Christmas
Eve – old Scrooge sat busy in his counting house. It was cold,
bleak, biting weather: foggy withal: and he could hear the people
in the court outside go wheezing up and down, beating their hands
upon their breasts, and stamping their feet upon the pavement

159

stones to warm them. The City clocks had only just gone three, but it was quite dark already – it had not been light all day – candles were flaring in the windows of the neighbouring offices, like ruddy smears upon the palpable brown air. The fog came pouring in at every chink and keyhole, and was so dense without, that, although the court was of the narrowest, the houses opposite were mere phantoms. To see the dingy cloud come drooping down, obscuring everything, one might have thought that nature lived hard by, and was brewing on a large scale.

The door of Scrooge's counting house was open, that he might keep his eyes upon his clerk, who in a dismal little cell beyond, a sort of tank, was copying letters. Scrooge had a very small fire, but the clerk's fire was so very much smaller that it looked like one coal. But he couldn't replenish it, for Scrooge kept the coalbox in his own room; and so surely as the clerk came in with a shovel, the master predicted that it would be necessary for them to part. Wherefore the clerk put on his white comforter, and tried to warm himself at the candle; in which effort, not being a man of strong imagination, he failed.

'A merry Christmas, uncle! God save you!' cried a cheerful voice. It was the voice of Scrooge's nephew, who came upon him so quickly that this was the first intimation he had of his approach.

'Bah!' said Scrooge, 'Humbug!'

He had so heated himself with rapid walking in the fog and frost, this nephew of Scrooge's, that he was all in a glow; his face was ruddy and handsome; His eyes sparkled, and his breath smoked again.

'Christmas a humbug, uncle!' said Scrooge's nephew. 'You don't mean that, I am sure?'

'I do,' said Scrooge, 'Merry Christmas! What right have you to be merry? What reason have you to be merry? You're poor enough.'

'Come then,' returned his nephew gaily. 'What right have you to be dismal? What reason have you to be morose? You're rich enough.' Scrooge, having no better answer ready on the spur of the moment, said, 'Bah!' again; and followed it up with 'Humbug!'

'Don't be cross, uncle!' said the nephew.

'What else can I be,' returned the uncle, 'when I live in such a world of fools as this? Merry Christmas! Out upon Merry Christmas! What's Christmas-time to you but a time for paying bills without money; a time for finding yourself a year older, and not an hour richer; a time for balancing your books, and having every item in 'em through a round dozen of months presented dead against you? If I could work my will,' said Scrooge indignantly, 'every idiot who goes about with "Merry Christmas" on his lips should be boiled with his own pudding, and buried with a stake of holly through his heart. He should!'

After

Running to the window, Scrooge opened it, and put out his head. No fog, no mist, clear, bright, jovial, stirring, cold; cold, piping for the blood to dance to; golden sunlight; Heavenly sky; sweet fresh air; merry bells. Oh, glorious! glorious!

'What's today?' cried Scrooge, calling downward to a boy in Sunday clothes, who perhaps had loitered in to look about him.

'Eh?' returned the boy with all his might of wonder.

'What's today, my fine fellow?' said Scrooge.

'Today!' replied the boy. 'Why, it's CHRISTMAS DAY.'

'It's Christmas Day!' said Scrooge to himself. 'I haven't missed it. The Spirits have done it all in one night. They can do anything they like. Of course they can. Hallo, my fine fellow!'

'Hallo!' returned the boy.

'Do you know the Poulterer's in the next street but one, at the corner?' Scrooge inquired.

'I should hope I did,' replied the lad.

'An intelligent boy!' said Scrooge. 'A remarkable boy! Do you know whether they've sold the prize turkey that was hanging up there? Not the little prize turkey, the big one?'

'What! the one as big as me?' returned the boy.

'What a delightful boy!' said Scrooge. 'It's a pleasure to talk to him. Yes, my buck!'

'It's hanging there now,' replied the boy.

'Is it?' said Scrooge. 'Go and buy it.'

'Walk-ER!' exclaimed the boy.

'No, no,' said Scrooge, 'I am in earnest. Go and buy it, and tell 'em to bring it here, that I may give them the directions where to take it. Come back with the man, and I'll give you a shilling. Come back with him in less than five minutes and I'll give you half-a-crown!'

The boy was off like a shot. He must have had a steady hand at a

161

trigger who could have shot off half so fast.

'I'll send it to Bob Cratchit's,' whispered Scrooge, rubbing his hands and splitting with a laugh. 'He shan't know who sends it. It's twice the size of Tiny Tim. Joe Miller never made such a joke as sending it to Bob's will be!'

The hand in which he wrote the address was not a steady one; but write it he did, somehow, and went downstairs to open the street-door, ready for the coming of the poulterer's man. As he stood there, waiting his arrival, the knocker caught his eye.

'I shall love it as long as I live!' cried Scrooge, patting it with his hand. 'I scarcely ever looked at it before. What an honest expression it has on its face! It's a wonderful knocker! – Here's the turkey! Hallo! Whoop! How are you? Merry Christmas!'

It was a turkey! He never could have stood upon his legs, that bird … he would have snapped 'em short off in a minute; like sticks of sealing-wax.

'Why, it's impossible to carry that to Camden Town,' said Scrooge, 'you must have a cab.'

The chuckle with which he said this, and the chuckle with which he paid for the turkey and the chuckle with which he paid for the cab, and the chuckle with which he recompensed the boy, were only to be exceeded by the chuckle with which he sat down breathless again in his chair, and chuckled until he cried.

Shaving was not an easy task, for his hand continued to shake very much; and shaving requires attention, even when you don't dance while you're at it. But, if he had cut the end of his nose off, he would have put a piece of sticking plaster over it, and been satisfied.

He dressed himself 'all in the best', and at last got out into the streets. The people were by this time pouring forth, as he had seen them with the Ghost of Christmas Present; and walking with his hands behind him, Scrooge regarded everyone with a delighted smile. He looked so irresistibly pleasant, in a word, that three or four good-humoured fellows said, 'Good morning, sir! A merry Christmas to you!' And Scrooge said afterwards that, of all the blithe sounds he had ever heard, those were the blithest to his ears.

THE NIGHT BEFORE CHRISTMAS

By Clement Clarke Moore

'Twas the night before Christmas, when all through the house
Not a creature was stirring, not even a mouse;
The stockings were hung by the chimney with care,
In hopes that St Nicholas soon would be there;
The children were nestled all snug in their beds,
While visions of sugar plums danced in their heads;
And mamma in her 'kerchief, and I, in my cap,
Had just settled our brains for a long winter's nap,
When out on the lawn there arose such a clatter,
I sprang from the bed to see what was the matter.
Away to the window I flew like a flash,
Tore open the shutters and threw up the sash.
The moon on the breast of the new fallen snow
Gave the lustre of mid-day to objects below,
When, what to my wondering eyes should appear,
But a miniature sleigh, and eight tiny reindeer,
With a little old driver, so lively and quick,
I knew in a moment it must be St Nick.
More rapid than eagles his coursers they came,
And he whistled, and shouted, and called them by name;
'Now, Dasher! now, Dancer! now Prancer and Vixen!
On, Comet! on, Cupid!, on, Donner and Blitzen!
To the top of the porch! to the top of the wall!
Now dash away! dash away! dash away all!'
As dry leaves that before the wild hurricane fly,
When they meet with an obstacle, mount to the sky;
So up to the house-top the coursers they flew,
With the sleigh full of toys, and St Nicholas too.
And then, in a twinkling, I heard on the roof
The prancing and pawing of each little hoof.
As I drew in my head, and was turning around,
Down the chimney St Nicholas came with a bound.
He was dressed all in fur, from his head to his foot,
And his clothes were all tarnished with ashes and soot;

A bundle of toys he had flung on his back,
And he looked like a pedlar just opening his pack.
His eyes – how they twinkled! his dimples how merry!
His cheeks were like roses, his nose like a cherry!
His droll little mouth was drawn up like a bow,
And the beard of his chin was as white as the snow;
The stump of a pipe he held tight in his teeth,
And the smoke it encircled his head like a wreath;
He had a broad face and a little round belly,
That shook when he laughed, like a bowlful of jelly.
He was chubby and plump, a right jolly old elf,
And I laughed when I saw him, inspite of myself;
A wink of his eye and a twist of his head,
Soon gave me to know I had nothing to dread.
He spoke not a word, but went straight to his work,
And filled all the stockings; then turned with a jerk,
And laying his finger aside of his nose,
And giving a nod, up the chimney he rose;
He sprang to his sleigh, to his team gave a whistle,
And away they all flew like the down of a thistle.
But I heard him exclaim, ere he drove out of sight,
'Happy Christmas to all, and to all a good night.'

CAROL
By anonymous medieval poet

I sing of a maiden
That is makeles;
King of all kings
To her son she ches.

He came al so still
There his mother was,
As dew in April
That falleth on the grass.

He came al so still
To his mother's bour,

As dew in April
That falleth on the flour.

He came al so still
There his mother lay,
As dew in April
That falleth on the spray.

Mother and maiden
Was never none but she;
Well may such a lady
Goddes mother be.

MRS RISLEY'S CHRISTMAS DINNER

By Ella Higginson

She was an old, old woman. She was crippled with rheumatism and bent with toil. Her hair was gray – not that lovely white that softens and beautifies the face, but harsh, grizzled gray. Her shoulders were round; her chest sunken; her face had many deep wrinkles. Her feet were large and knotty; her hands were large too, with great hollows running down their backs. And how painfully the cords stood out in her old, withered neck!

For the twentieth time she limped to the window and flattened her face against the pane. It was Christmas Day. A violet sky sparkled coldly over the frozen village. The ground was covered with snow; the roofs were white with it. The chimneys looked redder than usual as they emerged from its pure drifts and sent slender curls of electric blue smoke into the air.

The wind was rising. Now and then it came sweeping down the hill, pushing a great sheet of snow, powdered like dust, before it. The window-sashes did not fit tightly, and some of it sifted into the room and climbed into little cones on the floor. Snowbirds drifted past, like soft, dark shadows; and high overhead wild geese went sculling through the yellow air, their mournful 'hawnke-e-hawnk-hawnks' sinking downward like human cries.

As the old woman with her face against the window and her weak eyes strained down the street, a neighbour came to the door.

'Has your daughter an' her fambly come yet, Mis' Risley?' she asked, entering sociably.

'Not yet,' replied Mrs Risley, with a good attempt at cheerfulness; but her knees suddenly began shaking and she sat down.

'Why, she'd ought to 'a' come on the last train, hadn't she?'

'Oh, I don't know. There's plenty of time. Dinner won't be ready till past two.'

'She ain't been to see yer for five year, has she?' said the neighbour. 'I reckon you'll have a right scrumptious set-out fer 'em.'

'I will so,' said Mrs Risley, ignoring the other question. 'Her husband's comin'.'

Mrs Risley stooped to lay a stick on the fire.

'I've worked nigh on two weeks over this dinner,' she said, 'A-seedin' raisins and currants and things. I've hed to skimp harrable, Mis' Tomlinson, to get it; but it's jest – perfec'. Roast goose and cranberry sass, an' cel'ry soup, an' mince an' punkin pie – to say nothin' o' plum puddin'! An' cookies, an' cur'nt-jell' tarts fer the children. I'll hev to wear my old underclo's all winter to pay fer't; but I don't care.'

'I sh'u'd think your daughter'd keep you more comf'terble, seein' as her husband's so rich.'

There was a silence. Mrs Risley's face grew stern. The gold-coloured cat came and arched her back for a caress. 'My bread riz beautiful,' Mrs Risley said then. 'I worried so over it. An' my fruit cake smells that good, I put a whole cup o' brandy in it. Well, I guess you'll have to excuse me. I've got to set that table.'

When Mrs Tomlinson was gone the strained look came back into the old woman's eyes. She went on setting the table, but at the sound of every wheel or footstep she began to tremble and put her hand behind her ear to listen.

'It's funny they didn't come on that last train,' she said. 'I wouldn't tell her though, but they ought to be here by this time.'

She opened the oven door. The hot, delicious odour of its contents gushed out. Did ever a goose brown so perfectly before? And how large the liver was! It lay in the gravy in one corner of the big dripping-pan, just beginning to curl at the edges. She tested it carefully with a fork.

The mince-pie was on the table waiting to be warmed, and the pumpkin-pie was out on the back porch, from which the cat had been excluded at present. The cranberry sauce, the celery in its high, old-fashioned glass, the little beehive of hard sauce for the pudding, and the thick cream for the coffee bore the pumpkin-pie company. The currant jelly in the tarts glowed like great red rubies set in circles of old gold; the mashed potatoes were light as foam.

For one moment, as she stood there in the savoury kitchen, she thought of the thin, worn flannels, and of how much better her rheumatism would be with the warm ones which could have been bought with the money spent on this dinner. Then she flushed with self-shame.

'I must be gittin' childish in my old age,' she exclaimed indignantly, 'to begredge a Christmas dinner to my 'Lizy. 'S if I hedn't put up with old underclo's afore now! But I will say there ain't many women o' my age thet c'u'd get up a dinner like this 'n – rheumatiz 'n all.'

A long, shrill whistle announced the last train from the city. Mrs Risley started and turned pale. A violent trembling seized her. She could scarcely get to the window, she stumbled so. On the way to the window she stopped at the old walnut bureau to put a lace cap on her white hair and to look anxiously in the mirror.

'Five year!' she whispered. 'It's an offal spell to go wi'out seein' yer only daughter! Everythin'll seem might poor and shabby to her, I reckon – her old mother worst o' all. I never sensed how I'd changed 'til now. My! I'm all of a trimble!'

Then she stumbled on to the window and pressed her cheek against the pane.

'They'd ort to be in sight now,' she said. But the minutes went by and they did not come.

'Mebbe they've stopped to talk, meetin' folks,' she said, again. 'But they'd ort to be in sight now.' She trembled so she had to get a chair and sit down. But still she wrinkled her cheek upon the cold pane and strained her dim eyes down the street.

After a while a boy came whistling down from the corner. There was a letter in his hand. He stopped and rapped, and when she opened the door with a kind of frightened haste, he gave her the letter, and went away, whistling again.

A letter! Why should a letter come? Her heart was beating in her throat now – that poor old heart that had beaten under so many sorrows! She searched in a dazed way for her glasses. Then she fell helplessly into a chair and read it:

'DEAR MOTHER, – I am so sorry we cannot come, after all. We just got word that Robert's aunt has been expecting us all the time, because we've spent every Christmas there. We feel as if we must go there, because she always goes to so much trouble to get up a fine dinner; and we knew you wouldn't do that. Besides, she is so rich, and one has to think of one's children, you know. We'll come sure next year. With a merry, merry Christmas from all, ELIZA.'

It was hard work reading it, she had to spell out so many of the words. After she had finished she sat for a long, long time motionless, looking at the letter. Finally the cat came and rubbed against her, 'Meaowing' for her dinner. Then she saw that the fire had burned down to a grey, desolate ash.

She no longer trembled, although the room was cold. The wind was blowing steadily now. It was snowing, too. The bleak Christmas afternoon and the long Christmas night stretched before her. Her eyes rested on the little fir-tree on a table in one corner, with its gilt balls and strings of popcorn and coloured candles. She could not bear the sight of it. She got up stiffly.

'Well, kitten,' she said, trying to speak cheerfully, but with a pitiful break in her voice, 'let's go and eat our Christmas dinner.'

CHRISTMAS BELLS

By Henry Wadsworth Longfellow

I heard the bells on Christmas Day
Their old familiar carols play,
    And wild and sweet
    The words repeat
Of peace on earth, good-will to men.

And thought how, as the day had come,
The belfries of all Christendom
    Had rolled along
    The unbroken song
Of peace on earth, good-will to men!

Till, ringing, swinging on its way,
The world revolved from night to day,
A voice, a chime,
A chant sublime
Of peace on earth, good-will to men!

It was as if an earthquake rent
The hearth-stones of a continent,
And made forlorn
The households born
Of peace on earth, good-will to men!

And in despair I bowed my head;
'There is no peace on earth,' I said;
'For hate is strong,
And mocks the song
Of peace on earth, good-will to men!'

Then pealed the bells more loud and deep:
'God is not dead; nor doth He sleep!
The Wrong shall fail,
The Right prevail,
With peace on earth, good-will to men?'

CHRISTMAS AT GRECIO
By St Bonaventure,
Life of St Francis of Assisi

It happened in the third year before his death, that in order to
excite the inhabitants of Grecio to commemorate the nativity of the
infant Jesus with great devotion, he determined to keep it with all
solemnity; and lest he should be accused of lightness or novelty, he
asked and obtained the permission of the sovereign Pontiff. Then
he prepared a manger, and brought hay, and an ox and an ass to
the place appointed. The brethren were summoned, the people
ran together, the forest resounded with their voices, and that
venerable night was made glorious by many and brilliant lights
and sonorous psalms of praise. The man of God stood before the

169

manger, full of devotion and piety, bathed in tears and radiant with joy; many Masses were said before it, and the Holy Gospel was chanted by Francis, the Levite of Christ. Then he preached to the people around of the nativity of the poor King; and being unable to utter his Name for his tenderness of his love, he called Him the Babe of Bethlehem. A certain valiant and voracious soldier, Master John of Grecio, who, for the love of Christ, had left the warfare of this world, and become a dear friend of the holy man, affirmed that he beheld an Infant marvellously beautiful sleeping in that manger, Whom the blessed Father Francis embraced with both his arms, as if he would awake Him from sleep.

This vision of the devout soldier is credible, not only by the reason of the sanctity of him that saw it, but by reason of the miracles which afterwards confirmed its truth. For the example of Francis, if it be considered by the world is doubtless sufficient to excite all hearts which are negligent in the faith of Christ; and the hay of that manger, being preserved by the people, miraculously cured all diseases of cattle, and many other pestilences; God thus in all things glorifying His servant, and witnessing to the great efficacy of his holy prayers by manifest prodigies and miracles.

SANTA CLAUS

By Sophia Snow

'Twas the eve before Christmas; good-night had been said,
And Annie and Willie had crept into bed.
There were tears on their pillows, and tears in their eyes,
And each little bosom was heaving with sighs;
For to-night their stern father's command had been given
That they should retire precisely at seven
Instead of at eight; for they troubled him more
With questions unheard of than ever before.
He had told them he thought this delusion a sin;
No such creature as Santa Claus ever had been;
And he hoped, after this, he should never more hear
How he scrambled down chimneys with presents each year.

And this was the reason that two little heads
So restlessly tossed on their soft, downy beds.
Eight, nine, and the clock on the steeple toiled ten,
Not a word had been spoken from either till then;
When Willie's sad face from the blanket did peep,
And he whispered: 'Dear Annie, is 'ou fast asleep?'
'Why, no, brother Willie,' a sweet voice replies:
'I've long tried in vain, but I can't shut my eyes;
For somehow it makes me só sorry because
Dear papa has said there is no Santa Claus.
Now *we* know there is, and it can't be denied,
For he came every year before dear mama died;
But, then, I've been thinking that she used to pray, –
And God would hear everything mama would say, –
And maybe she asked him to send Santa Claus here
With the sack full of presents he brought every year.'
'Well, why tan'ot we p'ay, just as mama did, den,
And ask Dod to send him wis presents aden?'
'I've been thinking so, too;' and, without a word more,
Four bare little knees bounded out on the floor,
And four little knees on the soft carpet pressed,
And two tiny hands were close clasped to each breast; –
'Now, Willie, you know we must firmly believe
That the presents we ask for we are sure to receive;
You must wait just as still till I say the "Amen",
And by that you will know your time has come then. –
Dear Jesus, look down on my brother and me,
And grant us the favours we're asking of Thee.
I want a wax dolly, a tea-set and ring,
And an ebony workbox that shuts with a spring;
Bless papa, dear Jesus, and cause him to see
That Santa Claus loves us as much as does he;
Don't let him get fretful and angry again
At dear brother Willie and Annie. Amen.'

'Please, Desus, 'et Santa Taus tum down to-night,
And bring us some presents before it is 'ight;
I want he sood div' me a nice little sed,
With bright shinin' unners, and all painted 'ed;
A box full of tandy, a book and a toy,

Amen. And den, Desus, I'll be a dood boy.'
Their prayers being ended, they raised up their heads,
And with hearts light and cheerful, again sought their beds;
They were soon lost in slumber both peaceful and deep,
And with fairies in dreamland were roaming in sleep.
Eight, nine, and the little French clock had struck ten
Ere the father had thought of his children again;
He seems now to hear Annie's self-suppressed sighs,
And to see the big tears stand in Willie's blue eyes.
'I was harsh with my darlings,' he mentally said,
'And should not have sent them so early to bed;
But then I was troubled; my feelings found vent;
For bank stock today has gone down two per cent;
But, of course, they've forgotten their troubles ere this,
And that I denied them the thrice-asked-for-kiss;
But just to make sure, I'll steal up to their door –
To my darlings I never spoke harshly before.'

So saying, he softly ascended the stairs,
And arrived at the door to hear both of their prayers,
His Annie's 'Bless papa' drew forth the big tears,
And Willie's grave promise fell sweet on his ears.
'Strange, strange! I'd forgotten,' he said with a sigh,
'How I longed, when a child, to have Christmas draw nigh.
I'll atone for my harshness,' he inwardly said,
'By answering their prayers ere I sleep in my bed.'
Then he turned to the stairs and softly went down,
Threw off velvet slippers and silk dressing-gown,
Donned hat, coat and boots, and was out in the street,
A millionaire facing the cold, driving sleet!
Nor stopped he until he had bought everything,
From the box full of candy to the tiny gold ring.
Indeed, he kept adding so much to his store
That the various presents outnumbered a score.
Then homewards he turned, when his holiday load,
With Aunt Mary's help, in the nursery he stowed.
Miss Dolly was seated beneath a pine tree,
By the side of a table spread out for her tea;
A work-box, well filled, in the centre was laid,
And on it the ring for which Annie had prayed;

A soldier in uniform stood by a sled,
'With bright shining runners, and all painted red.'
There were balls, dogs, and horses; books pleasing to see;
And birds of all colours were perched in the tree;
While Santa Claus, laughing, stood up in the top,
As if getting ready more presents to drop.
Now, as the fond father the picture surveyed,
He thought for his trouble he'd amply been paid;
And he said to himself, as he brushed off a tear,
'I'm happier tonight than I've been for a year;
I've enjoyed more true pleasure than ever before,
What care I if bank stock fall two per cent more!
Henceforward I'll make it a rule, I believe,
That Santa Claus visit us each Christmas-eve.'
So thinking, he gently extinguished the light,
And, slipping downstairs, retired for the night.

As soon as the beams of the bright morning sun
Put the darkness to flight, and the stars one by one,
Four little blue eyes out of sleep opened wide,
And at the same moment the presents espied.
Then out of their beds they sprang with a bound,
And the very gifts prayed for were all of them found.
And they laughed and they cried, in their innocent glee;
And shouted for papa to come quick and see
What presents old Santa Claus brought in the night!
(Just the things they wanted!), and left before light.
'And now,' added Annie, in voice soft and low,
'You'll believe there's a Santa Claus, papa, I know;'
While dear little Willie climbed up on his knee,
Determined no secret between them should be,
And told, in soft whispers, how Annie had said
That their blessed mama, so long ago dead,
Used to kneel down and pray by the side of her chair,
And that God up in Heaven had answered her prayer.
'Den we dot up and p'ayed just as well as we tood,
And Dod answered our p'ayer, now wasn't He dood?'
'I should say that He was, if He sent you all these,
And knew just what presents my children would please.'
('Well, well, let him think so, the dear little elf!

173

'Twould be cruel to tell him I did it myself.')

Blind father! *who* caused your stern heart to relent,
And the hasty words spoken so soon to repent?
'Twas the Being who bade you 'steal softly upstairs',
And made you His agent, to answer their prayers.

RUPERT'S CHRISTMAS GIFT

By Bret Harte

We were all sitting in the drawing-room at Christmas, when the
doctor began – 'About four years ago, at this time I attended a
course of lectures in a certain city. One of the Professors invited
me to his house on Christmas night. I was very glad to go, as I was
anxious to see one of his sons, who, though only twelve years old,
was said to be very clever. Everybody predicted a splendid future
for him. Everybody but his father, for he was a very matter-óf-fact
man. There was a pleasant party that night. All the children of the
neighbourhood were there, and among them the Professor's clever
son, Rupert, as they called him, – a thin little chap, tall for his age,
fair and delicate. His health was feeble, his father said; he seldom
ran about and played with other boys, preferring to stay at home,
brood over his books, and compose what he called verses.

'Well, we had a Christmas tree, and we had all been laughing and
talking, calling the names of the children who had presents on the
tree, and everybody was very happy and joyous, when one of the
children suddenly called out, "Here's something for Rupert – and
what do you think it is?"

'We all guessed: – "A desk;" "A copy of Milton;" "A gold
pen;" "A rhyming dictionary;" "No? what then?"

' "A drum! With Rupert's name on it!"

'Sure enough there it was. A good-sized, bright, new,
brass-bound drum, with a slip of paper on it, with the inscription,
"FOR RUPERT."

'Of course we all laughed, and thought it a good joke. "You see
you're to make a noise in the world, Rupert!" said one. "Here's
parchment for the poet," said another. "Rupert's last work in
sheepskin covers," said a third. "Give us a classical tune, Rupert,"

said a fourth, and so on. But Rupert seemed too mortified to speak; he changed colour, bit his lips, and finally burst into a passionate fit of crying, and left the room. Then those who had joked him felt ashamed, and everybody began to ask who had put the drum there. But no one knew; though everybody declared that up to the moment it was produced, no one had seen it hanging on the tree. Rupert did not come downstairs again that night, and the party soon after broke up.

'I had almost forgotten those things, for the War of the Rebellion broke out the next spring, and I was appointed surgeon in one of the new regiments, and was on my way to the seat of war. But I had to pass through the city where the Professor lived, and there I met him. My first question was about Rupert. The Professor shook his head sadly. "He's not so well," he said; "he has been declining since last Christmas, when you saw him. A very strange case; but go and see him yourself; it may distract his mind and do him good." I went accordingly to the Professor's house, and found Rupert lying on a sofa, propped up with pillows. Around him were scattered his books, and, what seemed in singular contrast, that drum was hanging on a nail, just above his head. His face was thin and wasted; there was a red spot on either cheek, and his eyes were very bright and widely opened. He was glad to see me, and when I told him where I was going, he asked a thousand questions about the war. I thought I had thoroughly diverted his mind from its sick and languid fancies, when he suddenly grasped my hand and drew me toward him.

' "Doctor," he said, in a low whisper, "you won't laugh at me if I tell you something?"

' "No, certainly not," I said.

' "You remember that drum?" he said, pointing to the glittering toy that hung against the wall. "You know, too, how it came to me. A few weeks after Christmas, I was lying half asleep here, and the drum was hanging on the wall, when suddenly I heard it beaten; at first, low and slowly, then faster and louder, until its rolling filled the house. In the middle of the night, I heard it again. I did not dare tell anybody about it, but I have heard it every night since. Sometimes it is played softly, sometimes loudly, but always quickening to a long roll, so loud and alarming that I have looked to see people coming into my room to ask what was the matter. But I think, Doctor – I think – that no one hears it but myself."

175

'I thought so, too, but I asked him if he heard it at any other time.

' "Once or twice in the daytime," he replied, "when I have been reading or writing; then very loudly, as though it were angry, and tried in that way to attract my attention away from my books."

'I looked into his face, and placed my hand upon his pulse. His eyes were very bright and his pulse a little flurried and quick. I then tried to explain to him that he was very weak, and that his senses were very acute, as most weak people's are; and how that when he read, or grew interested and excited, or when he was tired at night, the throbbing of a big artery made the beating sound he heard. He listened to me with a sad smile of unbelief, but thanked me, and in a little while I went away. I left the city that very day, and in the excitement of battlefields and hospitals, I forgot all about little Rupert. Not long after we had a terrible battle, in which a portion of our army was slaughtered. When I reached the barn that served for a temporary hospital, I went at once to work.

'I turned to a tall, stout Vermonter, who was badly wounded in both thighs, but he held up his hands and begged me to help others first who needed it more than he. I did not at first heed his request, for this kind of unselfishness was very common in the army; but he went on – "For God's sake, Doctor, leave me here, there is a drummer-boy of our regiment – a mere child – dying, if he isn't dead now. Go and see him first. He lies over there. He saved more than one life. He was at his post in the panic this morning, and saved the honour of the regiment." I was so much impressed by the man's manner that I passed over to where the drummer lay, with his drum beside him. I gave one glance at his face – and – yes, it was Rupert.

'Well! Well! it needed not the chalked cross which my brother surgeons had left upon the rough board on which he lay to show how urgent was the relief he sought; it needed not the prophetic words of the Vermonter, nor the damp that mingled with the brown curls that clung to his pale forehead, to show how hopeless it was now. I called him by name. He opened his eyes – larger, I thought, in the new vision that was beginning to dawn upon him – and recognized me. He whispered, "I'm glad you are come, but I don't think you can do me any good."

'I could not tell him a lie. I could not say anything. I only pressed his hand in mine as he went on –

176

' "But you will see father, and ask him to forgive me. Nobody is to blame but myself. It was a long time before I understood why the drum came to me on Christmas night, and why it kept calling to me every night, and what it said. I know it now; the work is done, and I am content. Tell father it is better as it is. I should have lived only to worry and perplex him, and something in me tells me this is right."

'He lay still for a moment, and then, grasping my hand, said – "Hark!"

'I listened, but heard nothing but the suppressed moans of the wounded men around me. "The drum," he said, faintly; "don't you hear it? The drum is calling me."

'He reached out his arm to where it lay, as though he would embrace it.

' "Listen," he went on, "it's the reveille. There are the ranks drawn up in review. Don't you see the sunlight flash down the long line of bayonets? Their faces are shining – they present arms – there comes the General – but his face I cannot look at, for the glory round his head. He sees me; he smiles, it is –" and with a name upon his lips that he learned long ago, he stretched himself wearily upon the planks, and lay quite still.'

CHRISTMAS DAY IN THE WORKHOUSE

By George R.Simms

It is Christmas Day in the Workhouse,
And the cold bare walls are bright
With garlands of green and holly,
And the place is a pleasant sight:
For with clean-washed hands and faces,
In a long and hungry line
The paupers sit at the tables
For this is the hour they dine.

And the guardians and their ladies
Although the wind is east,
Have come in their furs and wrappers,

To watch their charges feast;
To smile and be condescending,
Put pudding on pauper plates,
To be hosts at the workhouse banquet
They've paid for – with the rates.

Oh, the paupers are meek and lowly
With their 'Thank'ee kindly, mum's'
So long as they fill their stomachs,
What matter it whence it comes?
But one of the old men mutters,
And pushes his plate aside:
'Great God!' he cries, 'but it chokes me!
For this is the day *she* died.'

The guardians gazed in horror,
The master's face went white;
'Did a pauper refuse the pudding?'
'Could their ears believe aright?'
Then the ladies clutched their husbands,
Thinking the man would die,
Struck by a bolt, or something,
By the outraged One on high.

But the pauper sat for a moment,
Then rose 'mid a silence grim,
For the others had ceased to chatter
And trembled in every limb.
He looked at the guardians' ladies,
Then, eyeing their lords, he said,
'I eat not the food of villains
Whose hands are foul and red:

'Whose victims cry for vengeance
From their dank, unhallowed graves.'
'He's drunk!' said the workhouse master,
'Or else he's mad and raves.'
'Not drunk or mad,' cried the pauper,
'But only a hunted beast,
Who, torn by the hounds and mangled,

Declines the vulture's feast.

'I care not a curse for the guardians,
And I won't be dragged away.
Just let me have the fit out,
It's only Christmas Day
That the black past comes to goad me,
And prey on my burning brain;
I'll tell you the rest in a whisper, –
I swear I won't shout again.

'Keep your hands off me, curse you!
Hear me right out to the end.
You come here to see how paupers
The season of Christmas spend.
You come here to watch us feeding,
As they watch the captured beast.
Hear why a penniless pauper
Spits on your paltry feast.

'Do you think I will take your bounty,
And let you smile and think
You're doing a noble action
With the parish's meat and drink?
Where is my wife, you traitors –
The poor old wife you slew?
Yes, by the God above us,
My Nance was killed by you!

'Last winter my wife lay dying,
Starved in a filthy den;
I had never been to the parish –
I came to the parish then.
I swallowed my pride in coming,
For, ere the ruin came,
I held up my head as a trader.
And I bore a spotless name.

'I came to the parish, craving
Bread for a starving wife,

Bread for the woman who'd loved me
Through fifty years of life;
And what do you think they told me,
Mocking my awful grief?
That "the House" was open to us,
But they wouldn't give "out relief".

'I slunk to the filthy alley –
'Twas a cold, raw Christmas eve –
And the baker's shops were open,
Tempting a man to thieve;
But I clenched my fists together,
Holding my head awry,
So I came to her empty-handed
And mournfully told her why.

'Then I told her "the House" was open;
She had heard of the ways of *that*,
For her bloodless cheeks went crimson,
And up in her rags she sat,
Crying, "Bide the Christmas here, John,
We've never had one apart;
I think I can bear the hunger, –
The other would break my heart."

'All through that eve I watched her,
Holding her hand in mine,
Praying the Lord, and weeping,
Till my lips were salt as brine.
I asked her once if she hungered,
And as she answered "No,"
The moon shone in at the window
Set in a wreath of snow.

'Then the room was bathed in glory,
And I saw in my darling's eyes
The far-away look of wonder
That comes when the spirit flies;
And her lips were parched and parted,
And her reason came and went,

For she raved of our home in Devon,
Where our happiest years were spent.

'And the accents long forgotten,
Came back to the tongue once more,
For she talked like the country lassie
I woo'd by the Devon shore.
Then she rose to her feet and trembled,
And fell on the rags and moaned,
And, "Give me a crust – I'm famished –
For the love of God!" she groaned.

'I rushed from the room like a madman,
And flew to the workhouse gate,
Crying, "Food for a dying woman!"
And the answer came, "Too late."
They drove me away with curses;
Then I fought with a dog in the street,
And tore from the mongrel's clutches
A crust he was trying to eat.

'Back through the filthy by-lanes!
Back, through the trampled slush!
Up to the crazy garret,
Wrapped in an awful hush.
My heart sank down at the threshold,
And I paused with a sudden thrill,
For there in the silv'ry moonlight
My Nance lay, cold and still.

'Up to the blackened ceiling
The sunken eyes were cast –
I knew on those lips all bloodless
My name had been the last;
She'd called for her absent husband –
O God! had I but known! –
Had called in vain, and in anguish
Had died in that den – alone.

'Yes, there in a land of plenty,

Lay a loving woman dead,
Cruelly starved and murdered
For a loaf of the parish bread.
At yonder gate, last Christmas,
I craved for a human life.
You, who would feast us paupers,
What of my murdered wife!

'There, get ye gone to your dinners;
Don't mind me in the least;
Think of the happy paupers
Eating your Christmas feast;
And when you recount their blessings
In your smug parochial way,
Say what you did for *me*, too,
Only last Christmas Day.'

THE CLOCK SPEAKS ON NEW YEAR'S EVE

By Paul West

Tick-tock! Tick-tock!

This is going to be an eventful evening. I feel it in every wheel and spring in my works.

She feels it too. See how ill at ease she is! How she listens to every sound without! How nervously she looks at me every two minutes!

Ah, pretty one, I know your secret!

Tick-tock! Tick-tock!

They are coming tonight, and you feel, you know, that before midnight you will have given your hand and your heart to one of them. But to which one?

I think I know. I am sure I know, even better than you, the one you prefer in your inmost heart.

He is poor; but the other night, when I had run down, he wound me and set me right.

The other one is rich; but last week, as he waited for you to dress for the theatre, he looked at me and swore because you were late. A man who will swear at a clock!

Tick-tock! Tick-tock!

There goes the bell!

Which do you suppose it is?

Oh, my dear, we are excited, you and I! Take one more glance at your lovely self in the mirror, though, goodness knows, you are always beautiful.

Tick-tock! Tick-tock!

Your novel, girl! Your novel! That's it. Don't let him know you are nervous. Now, rise to meet him.

Tick-tock! Tick-tock!

It's the poor one! But how handsome! Such a man! And flowers! Well, well! This does look well. Bride's roses, too. Here, don't –

Whew! I thought she was going to leave them right before me on the mantel! Then I couldn't have seen a thing.

Tick-tock! Tick-tock!

That's it. Two of the largest roses in your belt. That will encourage him.

Oh, I would not give a Waterbury watch for the rich one's chances now, if all goes right!

Tick-tock! Tick-tock!

Tick-tock! Tick-tock!

Still the weather, and the theatre, and the war; and the war, and the theatre, and the weather.

This will never do! Half-an-hour gone, thirty of the most precious minutes in your lives, and you are no nearer –

Tick-tock! Tick-tock!

Shades of Galileo! For what hour did the other, the rich one, make tonight's engagements? Wasn't it half-past-eight? It was! Ah, no wonder, pretty one, you start as you recall that, and look at me!

I cannot lie for you. It is eight-fifteen. And you have led him on not one single whit!

Tick-tock! Tick-tock!

Can you not perceive how bashful he is? Can you not divine, by the glances he casts at you, by his sighs, his awkwardness, how the land lies?

Tick-tock! Tick-tock!

You have only thirteen minutes, and then the other man will be here, and this one will have to go. And he will be broken-hearted.

Then the other one? Ah, he is business-like and cold-blooded. And he will ask you, and you will say yes.

Twelve minutes!

He is looking at you and clearing his throat to speak. Now help him. Look down at your roses, and if you can bring a little blush –

Oh, admirable! Admirable! You have given him courage, for you have shown him that you know.

Nine minutes!

Oh, my precious pair, you must hurry!

Tick-tock! T-i-i-i-ck-to-o-o-o-ck! I will try to run slowly, even at the cost of my reputation.   T-i-i-i-ck! To-o-o-o-ck!

He speaks! He says your name!

Look up! But not at him; that will frighten him. Say 'Yes?' and incline yourself a little toward him, as though to show your interest.

T-i-i-i-ck! To-o-o-o-ck!

Oh, you blundering man, do not look at me! I am doing my best for you, can't you see?

'How strange that clock sounds! As though' –

Ah, my girl! that was good.

He will finish the sentence!

'As though it wished to speak, almost. Ah, Elsa, I am like that clock, that would speak, but cannot! Elsa! Elsa!' Tick-tock! Tick-tock! Ticka-ticka-tocka-ticka-tock!

Hooray!

It is done!

But I must not look! I must cover my face with my hands!

THE NEW YEAR

By Lewis Novra

'The King is dead! Long live the King!'
  How oft those words renowned
Come back to me when joy bells ring
  With sweet and cheering sound!
Those bells that say, 'A year is dead!
  Another's King today!'
Aye, King, ere yet the echoing chime
  Of midnight dies away.

And though the wintry winds oft sing
  The dead King's funeral song,
We know that round the new-born King
  Spring flowers will bloom ere long.
Then be thy sorrows what they may,
  Let hope dispel each fear,
When all who meet thee, smiling, say,
  'A HAPPY, BRIGHT NEW YEAR!'

HANG UP THE BABY'S STOCKING!

Hang up the baby's stocking! Be sure
you don't forget! The dear little dimpled
darling, she never saw Christmas
yet! But I've told her all about it, and
she opened her big blue eyes; and I'm sure
she understood it – she looked so funny
and wise. Dear, what a tiny stocking!
It doesn't take much to hold such
little pink toes as baby's away from the
frost and cold. But then, for the baby's
Christmas, it will never do at all. Why!
Santa wouldn't be looking for anything
half so small. I know what will
do for the baby. I've thought of
the very best plan. I'll borrow a
stocking of Gran's, the longest
that ever I can. And you'll
hang it by mine, dear mother,
right here in the corner,
so! And leave a letter to
Santa, and fasten it on to
the toe. Write – this
is the baby's stocking,
that hangs in the corner
here. You never have
seen her, Santa, for she
only came this year
But she's just the blessed'st
baby. And now
before you go, just cram
her stocking with
goodies, from the
top clean down
to the
toe!

Mummers' Plays'

'Open the door and let us in, we hope your favour we shall win,
whether we rise, or whether we fall, we'll do our duty to please you
all;
Now acting time is come and we do here appear,
The time of mirth and merriment to all spectators here ...'

Performing plays in the winter was a practice begun by the early
races as a form of pagan ceremony rather than as a form of
entertainment. The Ancient Egyptians, Greeks and many early
races believed in magic. The winter months often brought famine
as the cold weather caused hardship and struggle for survival, and
their only hope was to look towards something mystical that
would improve the weather and so bring food. This was a period
when Mummers' plays began, and although none of the earliest
was written down, we know their origins and the plots because,
whatever the dialogue, the plot was always the same – two brave
men fight until the death of one of them, who is then brought back
to life by a quack doctor. He is always brought back for the good
of his people, and in many ways the simple Mummers' play is the
forerunner of that greatest epic of all where Christ died and came
back from the dead to save us.

Mummers' plays have been performed through the centuries
and were performed regularly throughout England at Christmas
until the outbreak of the First World War. Since that time their
popularity has waned, but in recent years many old scripts have
been revived as people cling even more to age-old traditions. At
one time almost every village had its own version of the Mummers'
play, and although every script differed from region to region, the
basic story always remained the same: the death of a hero (usually
St George) and his miraculous return to life. When it was
performed as a mystical ceremony people gave money to the
players to bring good luck; today staging a simple Mummers' play
can be a splendid way of raising money for charity.

Presented here is an ancient Westmorland version which was
performed by children going from door to door, just as we go carol
singing today. In those days they called it 'pace-egging' as the
children who performed the play were given an egg as a reward,
which of course meant food and survival. Because the plays were
performed from house to house, they were done without any kind
of scenery and very little costume. Traditionally Mummers wore
animal skins or suits made of straw or ribbons, and they often
blackened their faces as their identity had to be kept a secret if the
play was to bring good luck to the audience.

Today children perform Mummers' plays in schools and construct elaborate suits of armour and use imitation blood and the like, but this is unnecessary. To give the feel of old England, each member of the company can wear a smock or a simple cloak, and it's fun if the knights have imitation cardboard swords with which to fight, Devilty Doubt can have a broom and the doctor (Old Toss Pot) a doctor's bag. At the end Molly Masket and Old Toss Pot can go round with baskets or hats to collect money.

To perform this play today, combine it with carol singing. A few favourite carols can be sung before and after the play, and the play can be performed at any house at which you are invited in. It is a good idea to explain beforehand that you are going to perform a traditional Mummers' play, and an explanation of 'pace-egging' helps too. Something like this would be ideal:

'Good evening, Ladies and Gentlemen, and a very merry Christmas to you. In keeping with the ancient traditions of Christmas we would like to perform for you a short Mummers' play. The version we are to perform originated in Westmorland and was performed annually in and around Kirby Lonsdale up until 1910. As a reward the performers received eggs and beer, and the whole event was known as "pace-egging". We've come a-pace-egging for you tonight, but we hope that instead of being generous with your eggs, you will be generous with your money which will all be going to the —— [name of charity]. Thank you.'

Then everybody sings the opening song.

On this occasion it doesn't matter if Molly Masket is a man dressed as a woman (as frequently happened), and some of the characters can double if necessary; for example, Lord Nelson can double as St George.

MUMMERS' PLAY

(Nineteenth Century. Anon.)

Characters:

LORD NELSON	ST GEORGE
OLD TOSS POT	TURKISH KNIGHT
OLD PADDY	KING OF EGYPT
MALLY BROWN BAGS	DEVILTY DOUBT

INTRODUCER

Here's two or three jol-ly boys all in one mind, We've
come a-pace-egg-ing and hope you'll prove kind, We
hope you'll prove kind with your eggs and strong beer, We'll
come no more nigh you un———til the next year.
Fol de roo-dle di did-dle dum day,——— Fol de
roo-dle di did-dle dum day.———

Enter LORD NELSON. *Chorus sings:*

The first that comes in is Lord Nelson you see
With a bunch of blue ribbons tied down to his knee;
He's a star on his breast which like diamonds doth shine,
And he's come-a-pace-egging, it's pace-egging time.
(*Chorus*)

190

Enter JACK TAR. *Chorus sings:*

The next that you see is a Jolly Jack Tar
Who fought with Lord Nelson during the last war.
He's arrived from the sea Old England to view,
And has come a-pace-egging with our jolly crew.
(*Chorus*)

Enter OLD TOSS POT. *Chorus sings:*

The next that comes in is old Toss Pot you see,
He's a valiant old fellow in every degree.
He's a hump on his back and he wears a pig tail,
And all he delights in is drinking mulled ale.
(*Chorus*)

TOSS POT (*speaks*) In comes I a nivver come yet,
                Wi' me girt 'ead and me lill wit,
                And if me wit be nivver sae sma',
                Me and me pompey'll conquer you all.

Enter OLD PADDY. *Chorus sings:*

The next that comes in is old Paddy from York,
With his sickle and bundle he's come to seek work.
But work is so scarce it's compelled him to beg,
And he's come along wi' us to seek a Pace-egg.
(*Chorus*)

The next that comes in is old Mally Brown Bags,
She's so careful of money she goes in old rags.
She's gold and she's silver and copper in store
And she's come a-pace-egging and hopes to get more.
(*Chorus*)

Enter MALLY BROWN BAGS

MALLY MASKET   In comes I, old Mally Masket,
                    Under me arm I carries me basket,
                    In me basket I carries me eggs,
                    In pocket I drops me brass
                    And I think mesel' a jolly old lass.

Enter the DEVIL *with horns.*

DEVIL	In comes I Beelzebub,
	And on my shoulders I carry a club
	And in my hand a frying pan,
	And I think myself a jolly old man.

Enter DEVILTY DOUBT *with a hump and a broom.*

DEVILTY DOUBT	In comes I, old Devilty Doubt,
	If you don't give me something I'll sweep you all out.
	'Tis money I want and money I crave,
	Or I'll sweep all the lot of you into the grave.

Enter the TURKISH KNIGHT. *Chorus sings:*

The next that comes in is a bold Turkish Knight,
From a far distant country he's come for to fight.
He'll meet with St George and will fight with him here,
To show him a hero knows nothing to fear.
(*Chorus*)

INTRODUCER	Room, room, brave gallants, give us room to sport,
	For to this room we're wishful to resort.
	Resort, and to repeat our merry rhyme,
	Good sirs, remember it's pace-egging time.
	The time to go out pace-egging doth once again appear,
	So we come to act our play before you good folks here.
	Now that you hear the trumpet sound and hear us beat the drum,
	Make room, make room, brave gentlemen, and let our actors come.
ALL	We are the merry actors that travel through the street,
	We are the merry actors that all fight for our meat.
	We are the merry actors that show this pleasant play,
	So stir up the fire and strike a light, then –
	Step in St George and clear the way.

ST GEORGE   I am St George of England, that noble champion bold,
Who with my hands and sword did win three crowns of gold.
'Twas I that fought the fiery dragon and brought him to the slaughter
And by those means I also won the King of Egypt's daughter.
I've travelled all the world around and around,
But a man to equal me never have found.
Show me the man that dare before me stand!

TURKISH KNIGHT *steps forward and says:*

TURKISH KNIGHT   I am Black Prince of Paradise,
From Afric's land I came
On purpose to fight thee St George
Upon this very plain.
Of Black Morocco I am King, of fiery renown,
And with my sword I soon shall fetch thy lofty courage down.

ST GEORGE   Stand back, thou black Morocco dog,
Or by sword thou'lt die.
I'll cut thy body in four parts and make thy buttons fly.

TURKISH KNIGHT   Thou braggart, and thou boasting man,
That is not in thy power.
For I'll cut thee into slashes in less than half an hour.

ST GEORGE   Oh, slashing man! Oh slashing man! Don't tell so many lies,
For I'll cut thee into slashes as small as any flies
And send thee back across the sea to make into mince pies.
Mince pies hot, and mince pies cold,
I'll send thee to Black Sambo before thou'rt three days old.
Stand back thou black Morocco dog and let no

193

more be said,
For if I draw my glittering sword, I'll surely break thy head.

TURKISH KNIGHT How canst thou break my head,
When my head is made of brass and my body made of steel?
My legs and arms are knuckle bone, I'll challenge thee to feel.

ST GEORGE So! so! Bold Moor, neither boast nor stand,
But quickly draw and take thy sword in hand.
Let either one or both of us be slain,
Before we end and sheathe our swords again.

They start fighting. TURKISH KNIGHT *falls saying:*

TURKISH KNIGHT I am a bold and valiant knight and Slasher is my name,
Full many battles have I fought and always won the same,
But from St George I have received this bloody wound today.
Hark! Hark! The silver trumpets sound, I must no longer stay.

Enter KING OF EGYPT.

KING OF EGYPT I am the King of Egypt as plainly doth appear,
I've come to seek the young Black Prince who is my son and heir.
Who is the man who did him slay, his precious blood did spill,
Who is it that upon this ground my dearest son did kill?

ST GEORGE I did him slay, 'twas I that did him kill
And on this ground his precious blood did spill.
He challenged me to fight and why should I him deny?
Before I would a coward be I'd fight until I die.

KING OF EGYPT Oh, George! Oh George! What hast thou done?
Thou's gone and slain my only son,
Mine only son, mine only heir,

194

How can'st thou see him bleeding there?

MALLY MASKET	A Doctor! A Doctor! Ho, ho! What ho for a doctor!
TOSS POT	Here I am, a Doctor, but I will not come to thee under ten pounds.
KING OF EGYPT	I'll give ten, fifteen, twenty pounds for a Doctor!
TOSS POT	I am an actor, too.
KING OF EGYPT	I don't want an actor, I want a doctor! Art thou a doctor?
TOSS POT	I am a Jack of all trades.
MALLY MASKET	How can'st thou be a Jack of all trades?
TOSS POT	By my travels.
MALLY MASKET	How far hast thou travelled?
TOSS POT	I have travelled all up and down the country in this sort of manner and that. I have travelled from my grandmother's bedside to the fireside and from the fireside to the cupboard side where I have got many a lump of mouldy cheese and pie crust which made me such a rollicking, bullocking sort of boy as I am.
MALLY MASKET	Is that all?
TOSS POT	No! I have travelled round Italy, Spitally, France and Spain, all round England and back again.
MALLY MASKET	Can'st thou cure this poor man?
TOSS POT	Aye, I can cure him as thou shalt quickly see.
MALLY MASKET	What can'st thou cure?
TOSS POT	I can cure the itch, the stitch, the palsy and the gout,
	The plague within and the plague without.
	And if there be nineteen devils in that man's skull,
	I'll surely cast twenty of them out.

195

MALLY MASKET   Is that all?

TOSS POT   No! If you bring me an old woman of eight score eight,
Let her chin and her nose be both of a height,
I'll make her as pretty as that damsel over there.
(*Points at some girl.*)

MALLY MASKET   Is that all?

TOSS POT   No! As I was going through St Paul's Churchyard
Even the very dead came running after me saying,
'Doctor! Doctor! Give me one of your never failing pills,
It's a pity that such a man as I should have died.'

MALLY MASKET   Is that all?

TOSS POT   No! I've got in my pocket spectacles for blind bumble bees, crutches for lame ducks, pack saddles for grasshoppers and many other useful things.

MALLY MASKET   Is that all?

TOSS POT   No! I've got a bottle in my inside, outside, rightside, leftside waist-coat pocket, which my grandmother sent me from Spain three days after she died, that will surely bring any dead man back to life again. Why! I cured Sir Harry of a disease twenty yards long, and surely I can cure this poor man of his disorder.

Kneels down and hands the wounded man a bottle.

Here Jack, take a drop of this my nip nap,
Let it run down thy tip tap.
Now, if thou art not entirely slain,
Rise up and fight again.

The TURKISH KNIGHT *drains the bottle,*
stands up and shouts:

196

TURKISH KNIGHT	Oh! My back!
TOSS POT	What now is amiss with thy back?
TURKISH KNIGHT	My back is bound, my sword is sound, I'll have St George another round.
TOSS POT	Stop! Stop those swords without delay, And fight it out another day.

All form up in a ring and sing:

Now ladies and gentlemen that sit round the fire,
Put your hands in your pockets, that's all we desire.
Put your hands in your pockets and pull out your purse
And give us a trifle, you'll not feel much worse.

TOSS POT *then collects the money in his hat and*
MALLY MASKET *goes round with her basket for*
eggs. The performers were usually given refreshments
and 'summat to sup'.

Nativity Plays

Around the Middle Ages, Miracle Plays, sometimes known as Mystery Plays, became popular. These were always based on religious stories, often depicting the life of Christ from birth to death. Every four years medieval Mystery Plays are performed in York, usually amid the ruins of St Mary's Abbey, and certainly recapture the power and spirit of medieval drama. Just as medieval performers relied on nature for their lighting, so do modern actors in York, and it is uncanny how there is often the most incredibly beautiful sunset just at the moment of the crucifixion.

At Christmas, quite naturally, nativity plays were performed, often with a number of scenes from the visit of the Angel Gabriel to Mary to the journey of the Three Kings. Often these would be performed on successive nights, ending with the Massacre of the Innocents on Twelfth Night.

Here is part of a medieval miracle play 'translated' into more easily spoken English by Anne Malcolmson von Storch, originally for twelve-year-old children to perform, but this version can just as easily be performed by two adults and could be made a very moving part of a carol service, or simply performed before family and friends on Christmas Eve. Many nativity plays have a cast of thousands and can be seen in a million schools every Christmas; this script makes a refreshing change and can be powerfully performed by two actors.

The setting and costumes can be as elaborate as finances and resources allow, but as a story of such simplicity it works perfectly with no set or props other than a doll for the Christ Child and a wooden box of straw for the manger. Anything else can be mimed and left to the audience's imagination. If facilities allow, some very moving and dramatic lighting changes can help to create the right atmosphere. If the stage is dimly lit and then gradually Mary and the Baby become brilliantly lit by a single spotlight as she takes hold of the baby for the first time, it can say more than words ever can.

THE NATIVITY

From the York NATIVITY Play
(Medieval, adapted by Anne Malcolmson)

Characters: MARY

JOSEPH

The scene is laid outside a stable in Bethlehem. The stable is darkened at the opening of the play but later will be lighted to provide a traditional manger setting for Mary and the Christ Child. Mary and Joseph enter wearily. They see the stable. Mary waits downstage while Joseph examines the shed; then he comes to the centre of the stage and prays.

JOSEPH: Almighty God in Trinity,
I pray Thee, Lord, in Thy Great might,
Look down. Thy simple servant see.

Here in this place where we are brought,
Weak and alone.
Grant us a resting place this night
Within this town.

For we have sought both up and down,
Through diverse streets of this city!
So many people are come to town
That we can find no hostelry.
There is such a rabble,
Forsooth, no other help I see
But this poor stable.

(Joseph goes backstage, enters the dark stable, and looks it over carefully. He returns discouraged. He points out its defects to Mary as he speaks to her.)

If we here all night abide,
The storm will blow upon us still.
The walls are down on every side'
The roof is open to rain and hail
Above, I trow.
Say, Mary, daughter, what is thy will?
What shall we do?
For now we are in grievous need,
As thou thyself the sooth may see;
For here is neither blanket nor bed,
And we are weak and both weary,
And fain would rest.

(He turns away from her and prays again.)

Now, Gracious God, in Thy mercy,
Show what is best!

(Mary comes over to Joseph and speaks to him quietly and with confidence.)

MARY: God will guide us, full well know ye!
Therefore, Joseph, be of good cheer.
In this same place born will He be
That shall us save from sorrows sore,
Both night and morn.

Sir, know ye well, the time is near
When He will be born.

JOSEPH: Then it behooves us bide here still,
Here in this same place all this night.

MARY: Yea, forsooth, that is God's will.

(Joseph looks at her gently, then starts to make the stable comfortable, determined to make the best of things.)

JOSEPH: Then would I fain we had some light,
Whatever befall.
It grows right dark unto my sight,
And cold withal.

I will go get us light therefore,
And find some fuel to make a fire.

MARY: Almighty God, go you before,
As He is Sovereign of all things here,
In His great power!
May He lend me grace now to prepare
For this His hour!

(Joseph leaves the stage. Mary enters the stable. There is a pause. The outer stage is darkened, if possible, and suddenly the interior of the stable is lighted, to show Mary seated beside the manger, holding the child in her lap. She worships him.)

Hail! My Lord God! Hail, Prince of Peace!
Hail, my Father! And hail, my Son!
Hail, Sovereign Liege, all sins to cease!
Hail, God and Man, dwelling in One!
Hail, Thou, through whose might
All this world was first begun,
Darkness and Light!

Son, as I am subject of Thine,
Vouchsafe, sweet Son, now here I pray Thee,
That I may hold Thee in these arms of mine,
And in these poor weeds to array Thee.
Grant me but this,
As I am chosen Thy mother to be
In truthfulness!

(She wraps her cloak around the baby. Joseph enters downstage, carrying a lantern and some wood. He does not see the scene in the stable, but speaks directly to the audience.)

JOSEPH: Ah! Lord in Heaven! The weather is cold!
 The fearfullest freeze that I ever did feel!
 I pray God give succour to them that are old,
 And also to them that may be unwell,
 So I may say.
 Now, God, be Thou my Shelter still,
 As best Thou may!

(A star blazes out above the stable. He sees it and is startled.)

 Ah, Lord of All! What light is this
 That comes shining thus suddenly?
 I cannot say, as I have bliss!
 When I have brought this wood to Mary
 Then shall I inquire.

(He turns and sees the stable.)

 Thanks be to God, the place I see.

(He enters the stable.)

MARY: You are welcome, sir!

(Joseph speaks as he puts down the lantern and the wood.)

JOSEPH: Tell me, Mary daughter, how farest thee?

MARY: Well, Joseph, as has been aye.

(Joseph straightens up and suddenly seems to realize what has happened.)

JOSEPH: Oh, Mary, what sweet Thing is upon thy knee?

MARY: It is my Son, the sooth to say,
 That is so mild.

(Joseph falls to his knees in wonder.)

JOSEPH: Blessed am I, who am bade this day
 To see this Child.

(He worships for a moment, then half rises and looks about him.)

201

I marvel much at this light
That shineth thus throughout this place.
Forsooth, it is a wondrous sight!

MARY: This has He ordained of His grace,
My Son and King,
That a star be shining for a space
At his bearing.

For Balaam long ago foretold
How that full high should rise a star;
And of a maid should be born a Child,
A Son, that shall be our Saviour
From cares unkind.
Forsooth, it is my Son so free
Balaam bore in mind.

JOSEPH: Now, welcome, flower of the fairest hue!
I shall Thee worship with main and might.
Hail, my Maker! Hail, Christ Jesu!
Hail, royal King, Root of all right!
Hail, Saviour!
Hail, my Lord, Lender of light!
Hail, blessed Flower.

MARY: (*Speaking to the Child*)
Now, Lord, That all this world shall win –
To Thee, my Son, this must I say, –
Here is no cradle to lay Thee in.
Therefore, my dear Son, I Thee pray,
Since it is so,
That in this crib I may Thee lay,
Between beasts two.

(*She lays the child in the manger very gently and wraps her cloak around Him.*)

And I shall wrap Thee, my own dear Child,
With such poor clothes as we may have.

(*As Mary is attending to the Child, Joseph looks behind the manger. He turns and speaks to her in amazement.*)

JOSEPH: O Mary, behold these creatures mild!

They make devotions, loving and grave,
As if they were men!
Forsooth, it seems well and clearly told
That their Lord they ken.

MARY: Their Lord they ken, that know I well;
They worship Him with might and main.
The weather is cold, as ye may feel.
To cherish Him they are full fain.
With their breath warm
They breathe upon Him, this may you tell,
To keep Him from harm!

(*Mary looks back into the crib.*)

O, now sleeps my Son! Blest may He be!
He lies full warm these beasts between.

JOSEPH: Thus is fulfilled, forsooth I see,
What Habakkuk long ago did mean
In his prophesying.

He said our Saviour should be seen
Between beasts lying.

And now I see the same in sight.

MARY: Yea, forsooth, the same is He.

JOSEPH: Honour and worship both day and night,
Eternal Lord, be done to Thee,
As it is worthy.
And, Lord, to Thy service I promise me
With my heart wholly.

(*Joseph steps back from the crib and falls to his knees. Mary speaks in prayer, very slowly and clearly.*)

MARY: Thou merciful Maker, God on High,
Lord of Heaven, my Son so free,
Thy handmaiden, forsooth, am I;
And to Thy service I promise me,
With all my heart and mind.
And, Son, Thy blessing, beseech I Thee,
Thou grant to us, all mankind!

The Pantomime

'Oh yes it is! Oh no it isn't!'

One of the greatest dramatic inventions at Christmas was the pantomime, and for many people Christmas just wouldn't be Christmas without a visit to that uniquely British institution. Nowhere else in the world has this delightful hotch-potch of characters that can hop happily from one pantomime to another, where somebody's mother is a man dressed as a woman, and the heroine usually marries a prince who is a girl dressed as a boy!

Pantomime, as we know it, more or less, has been around for the last two hundred years. The Romans, of course, had a form of pantomime, but they wore masks and were scantily clad as a rule. Entertaining though this may have been, it's not what traditionalists call pantomime! The first pantomimes we would recognize as such came towards the end of the eighteenth century and were based on fairy stories.

By the nineteenth century, pantomime was in its heyday and had begun to develop into the burlesque comedy that we know today, a show that created a magical world of make-believe. The dame had arrived too, and in 1860 the great H.J. Byron wrote *Aladdin* and created the much-loved Widow Twankey. (It is believed that the name comes from ships called 'twankays' that brought tea to Britain from the Far East. It was probably the equivalent of calling her 'Mother Barge' or 'Mrs Battleship'.)

One gem that H.J. Byron penned soon after *Aladdin* didn't have quite the same impact, even though it was performed at Covent Garden in 1868. It was called *Robinson Crusoe* or *Friday and the Fairies*. If you want to perform a pantomime yourself, you could do worse than perform this one. It is an outrageous period piece.

With a cast of eight you can perform it in your own home, or if you really want to aim for the big time, with a few simple sets and costumes and a little ingenuity, you can hire a hall and attempt a public performance!

'Oh no you can't! Oh yes *you can*!'

ROBINSON CRUSOE

or FRIDAY AND THE FAIRIES!

a comical burlesque extravaganza in four scenes

by
Henry James Byron

Cast in Order of Appearance:

THE ELF	QUASHIBUNGO, Lord Chamberlain
THE SEDATE FAIRY	of the Cannibal Islands
ROBINSON CRUSOE	HOKYPOKYWANKYFUM, King
MRS CRUSOE	of the Cannibal Islands
FRIDAY	THE FAVOURITE SQUAW

FAIRIES, CHILDREN & SAVAGES

Scene I

The Enchanted Isle

(*Seated in his Nautilus Shell,* THE ELF *arrives. He lands, gazes about him in delight, and addresses the audience.*)

ELF: Well here we are again, I'm me, myself.
A tricksy, wicked, laughing, chaffing elf.
I've run away from Ma, and from our Grotto,
Of which she's queen – she'll wonder where I've got to,
For by this time, I've very little doubt,
My mother's quite aware that I am out.
This island is enchanted, and on here
There dwells a certain fairy, such a dear!
But oh! so proper, and oh! so severe.
She has been crossed in love, and won't admit
A male to touch this shore – but stop a bit,
I am a male – my resolution's stout,

And no malevolence shall keep me out;
I'll sing to catch their ears, howe'er she scold,
My singing's rather catching I've been told.

> Come as I raise my finger,
>   Come from each fairy grot;
> Lazily do not linger,
>   But with all speed you've got.
> Come from each fairy bower,
>   Come from each fairy dell,
> For I have just half-an-hour
>   To dance with each fairy-belle.
> Come pretty fays, come hither,
>   Beautiful, bashful, and coy;
> Come let us be happy together,
>   I'm only an innocent boy!

(*During this, Fairies from all sides appear and gather around him.
The* ELF *enchanted, addresses them.*)

> You ducks, you pretty dears, I've often watched you;
> And now, to use a vulgar rhyme, I've cotched you.
> Do dance for me, as for compunction – drop it.
> Do skip it, trip it – and do hop it – poppet.

Ballet:

*The Frolic of the Fairies**

(*At the end there is a slight rumbling of thunder and the fairies
group together in fear.*)

ELF: What's that?

(*Enter the* SEDATE FAIRY, *enraged.*)

S. FAIRY: What's that! Why, which it's me, vile scapegrace.

ELF: Your eyes are stars, lips rubies, and your shape grace,
          Beauty personified, come, don't look cross.
          To our society you're such a loss,
          Why shut yourself up here?

---

* When produced in the home, the Fairy Ballet is optional.

S. FAIRY: I've vowed a vow
Against the other sex. There'll be a row
If, sir, again you put your foot on here.

ELF: You can't get on without us, can you, dear?

S. FAIRY: What do you say! Be off! if not this minute,
I have a prison, and I'll pop you in it.

ELF: Of course, because you're loth to let me go.

S. FAIRY: I choke with rage – don't make of me your foe.

ELF: I'm going, but defy you here I do.
Listen the lot of you – it's very true
Your mistress has declared and vowed no male
Shall set foot on this island – don't turn pale,
Don't tremble, but remember what I've said
When crowds of individuals shall tread
This sacred soil – yes, shoals!

S. FAIRY Oh, I shall sink.

ELF: Of an invasion you are on the brink.
This island shall be over-run with men,
Since you won't let an Elf come now and then,
Until it doth resemble (how she quails!)
The General Post-Office – one mass of males.

(*The* ELF *runs to Nautilus, turns and defiantly threatens his antagonist the* S. FAIRY, *and the group of Nymphs and Fays around her. The curtain falls.*)

Scene II

A Street in Wapping

(ROBINSON CRUSOE *enters wheeling a perambulator and surrounded by his family.*)

ROB. C: What are you at? the baby would you smother!

MRS C (*without*): Robinson!

ROB. C: Now you'll catch it. Here's your mother.

(*Enter* MRS CRUSOE, *out of breath.*)

MRS C: You vagabond to go so fast, you wretch,
     You know well I my breath can scarcely fetch,
     Being asthmatical. The child you're dropping.
     I'm the forlornest woman in all Wapping.
     Oh! if I had a brother.

ROB. C: Wish you had,
     'Cos p'raps you'd go and live with him.

MRS C: You bad
     Ungrateful monster, you, oh! oh!

(*She clasps a hand to her side.*)

ROB.C: Now then,
     What is it?

MRS C: Oh! the spasms come again.

(*She pulls out a bottle.*)

ROB. C: Oh! oh!

MRS C: Well what's the matter, pray, with you?

ROB C: You've got the spasms, and I've got 'em too.
     One little drop.

MRS C (*shows empty bottle*):   All gone.

ROB. C: What all the lot?
     That's cool.

MRS C: Come home, sir, and you'll get it hot.
     There's nothing in the larder, go and work.
     You treat your poor wife like a downright Turk.
     Come on, my precious pets.

ROB. C: Be off.

MRS C (*shuddering contempt at him she collects the children and exits*):
     Bother!

ROB. C: Bother!
           The babies are noosance, so's their mother.

(*The* ELF *suddenly appears dressed as a sailor.*)

ELF: I've come here in a second and a half!
           'Twould puzzle the electric telegraph!

ROB. C (*meditating*):   To run, or not to run? That is the question.

ELF (*slapping him on the shoulder*):
           Run by all means, it's good for the digestion;
           You're miserable at home. Your wife's a tartar,
           You could not find more hardships on the warter.
           Come, go to sea.

ROB. C: Go to see what?

ELF: The Ocean.

ROB. C: The Ocean! not by no means a bad notion.

ELF: Let's have a little drop of something – quick!

(*A bottle appears.*)

ROB. C: Gracious! what's that?

ELF: Only the bottle trick.
           How do you like it?

ROB. C (*after drinking*):   G'lopshus.

ELF: Ain't it heady.

ROB. C (*staggers*): No, not a bit, now Robinson, stand steady.
           It's nectar.

ELF: Yes, we've got him, he's the man,
(*aside*): The very chap to carry out my plan.

(MRS CRUSOE, *with the children rushes on.*)

MRS C   Where is my husband? Where's my Robin-sun?
           From his fond wife he's been and cut and run.
           I want new clothes, the children want 'em too.
           The baker's troublesome, the rent is doo.
           The butcher's cut our legs off and the grocer

For his own raisons stopped our currents flow, sir.
We are afloating on a sea of troubles,
The greengrocer has stopped our vegetables.
A helpless woman's lone condition scorning,
Two executions have come in this morning.
Our water's cut off by a man in blue,
And now my Robinson is cut off too.
Where is he! *(sees him)*   Ha!

ELF: Now be prepared for breezes.

MRS C: He's there – yes, him I sees and him I seizes!

(MRS CRUSOE *chases her husband, who runs away accompanied by the* ELF, *as the curtain falls.*)

Scene III

The Enchanted Isle

(*Enter the* SEDATE FAIRY *in a furious temper.*)

S. FAIRY: Hang out our banners – no you don't mean that
You little, silly, stupid, fairy flat!
The cry is still they come, men creatures – lots,
A boatful of male human wretches blots
The landscape I have loved to look on free
From the vile presence of a single 'he'.
What's to be done? I have it. I'll invoke
My trusty vassals; Ha! my hearts of oak
Don't hope a footing on this shore to gain.
Wind come at once, and your accomplice, Rain!
How de do, Wind, Rain, how de do? my dear
Thunder and Lightning, instantly appear.
'Blow wind and crack your cheeks,' Rain fall in showers,
Thunder exhibit all your bolting powers,
Lightning please prove as flashing as you can
Remember your Queen's enemy is man;
Let not a single male in yonder vessel
Successfully against your powers wrestle,
with an o'rwhelming storm the rash fools greet,

And let the ocean be their winding sheet.

(*The storm breaks.*)

> They have obeyed their fairy monarch's wishes,
> Their victims now are food for little fishes;
> The hungry sea has swallowed up the lot,
> And I have triumphed.

(ELF *bounds in.*)

ELF: No, my dear, you've not,
As for your storm, I feel the utmost scorn for it,
For Crusoe'll never drown, he wasn't born for it,
Just keep your eye on that, and not on me,
And shortly you shall see, what you shall see,
He by his cunning has contrived a craft,
Better known as Robinson Crusoe's raft!

S. FAIRY   But he shan't triumph. If he is to land,
'Twill be to meet with foemen, understand,
You think this island uninhabited?
But you shall find out your mistake; instead,
I will import a race of savages,
Experts at fights, routs and ravages.

ELF: The gallant tar I've rescued from the water,
Is game for pitch and toss up to manslaughter!
Any excitement he's prepared for quite,
So it's agreed. We go in for a fight.

S. FAIRY: We do! To arms!

ELF: As sure as eggs is eggs,
'Stead of two arms, you'd better trust to legs!

(*They depart as* ROBINSON CRUSOE *enters.*)

ROB. C: Why did I go to sea? Why was I wrecked?
'Twas just the sort of thing I might expect.
Ill luck has followed me all through my life,
I used to have such rows with my poor wife.
She used to thrash me so, when I would let her,
I was much struck with her when I first met her.
Still her devoted husband she might whack again,

If to Old England he could but go back again,
Ha! ha! what's here? a human footprint surely.
Oh dear! oh dear! I feel uncommon poorly.
It's plain some one's been here – a human hoof –
Of course, it's evident; that's print's a proof.

(*A noise is heard without.*)

What's that? Who's them? Canoes! It's well I've got
A fowling piece, and powder, likewise shot.
They're not so civilised as yet to know
The way we wholesale can destroy a foe!

(*A war whoop is heard and* ROB. C *hastily conceals himself.* FRIDAY *rushes on terrified and falls exhausted, his pursuers following him.*)

(*Enter* QUASHIBUNGO *and two savages. They are about to kill* FRIDAY *when* ROB. C *from his concealment fires at them. They start and exhibit the greatest astonishment. He repeats the shot and with a frantic yell two of the savages fly in alarm and terror. He again fires, and* QUASH, *departs with a cry and a wound.* FRIDAY *and* ROB. C *approach each other with suspicion and caution, at length* FRIDAY *taking courage prostrates himself on the ground at* ROB. C*'s feet, placing as a mark of gratitude and submission, one foot on his shoulder.* ROB. C *playfully pushes him over.*)

ROB. C: An Englishman, my friend, does not make slaves
Of those poor individuals he saves.
You shall my servant be, shall hunt and shoot,
Nature provides you with a nice black suit,
It fits you like your skin – your wages clear
Will be-a-nothing-and, of course no beer;
You'll have no followers – no Sundays out,
There are no nursemaids you can take about;
My ease with Rasselas, doth somewhat tally,
And you must try to be, the happy valley.
Since today I've found you quite without a name,
I'll call you Friday, if it's all the same.
And now to feed – make a pie, good Friday.
Friday with me's invariably pie day.

(ROB. C *and* FRIDAY *make a pie, and then indulge in a popular Quadrille as the curtain falls.*)

Scene IV

Another part of the Island

(*Enter* SEDATE FAIRY.)

S. FAIRY: I'll punish him, but how? I've tried to think
Until of blank despair I've reached the brink.
What can I do? My plan's completely failed,
And warrior-like the isle's all over mailed.
The creatures I detect o'errun the shore,
From the white Briton to the blackamoor.

(*A large block of stone assumes human features.*)

I will consult the oracle. Look here,
What I'm to do is not precisely clear.
How can I punish Crusoe? Tell me what
Will be to him a sad and weary lot,
Something most dire, to cut him like a knife.
I wait your answer. Speak!

ORACLE (*opening mouth*): Send for his wife.

S. FAIRY: Send for his wife! That punishment's severe,
But it's deserved, so Mrs C. appear.

(MRS CRUSOE *enters*)

Good, and as luck will have it, he is here.

(SEDATE FAIRY *disappears. Enter* CRUSOE, *laughing.* MRS CRUSOE *takes her husband by the ear.*)

ROB. C: Well, this is downright jolly! I say, mum,
I know that finger and I know that thumb.

(ROB. C *and* MRS C *embrace. At this juncture they are surrounded by the Indians.*)

MRS C: Murder!

QUASH: Yar! yar! De king unfornnately,
          Hab not had any white folk to eat lately;
          You rader tough no doubt, but dat don't matter,
          We'll feed you up until you both get fatter.
          Seize 'em, and to our monarch dem ere bring,
          A dainty dish to set before de king.

The Grand Procession of the Tribes

(*The* KING *and* ROYAL SQUAW *drawn in state dragon chariot, by alligators.*)

HOKY: Bress you, my chibberlins. Few remarks just cussory,
          We will now make upon this annivussary,
          Ob our assuming dis here throne. My dears,
          We've been your sobberin a dozen years.
          We've raised your taxes, and increased your rent,
          Built sebberal prisons at our own expense.
          Incarcerated all as spoke dere mind,
          Determined to benefit mankind,
          By shutting up de schools, for dey alarm me,
          Pulled down the hospitals, increased the army,
          Warned liberals dat dey'll get in a mess,
          Hung all de radicals, and gagged the press,
          In fact come out in a parental way,
          Worthy de era and ob your hooray.

(*All shout 'Hooray'!*)

          Where am de pris'ners?

QUASH: Behold 'em, Sire.

HOKY: Tell dat dere cook to make a first-rate fire.
          Mind dat it's clear – no smoke.

MRS C: What does he mean?

HOKY: And take care dat de saucepan's berry clean.

ROB. C: I smell a rat. Oh, where shall we all go to?

MRS C: You smell a rat – som-ouse, Sir. I do so, too!
          The King's a hogling me.

214

(HOKY *comes down, admiring* MRS C, *who coquets.*)

HOKY: You pretty thing,
Ob all dese parts round here, I am de king,
Monarch of all dat I survey – you see.

MRS C: Begging your parding, which you're not of me.
I'm married –

HOKY: More de pity. I could eat you.

MRS C: To a good thrashing I should like to treat you.
Your wife's a looking.

HOKY: Wife! I got a dozen.

(*He puts his arm around* MRS C's *waist. The* SQUAW *is now making overtures to* ROB. C.)

SQUAW (*ogling him*): You do so much remind me of my cousin.

ROB. C: (*digs her in the ribs*): Ha! go along.

SQUAW: You are so lovely.

ROB. C: Yes,
I do show up these natives I confess.

SQUAW (*melo-dramatically.*): If you would kill the king and run
away with me?

ROB. C: But dearest, would you promise not to stay with me?
(*aside*) I don't mind taking old King Hoky's life,
But shouldn't so much care to take his wife.

HOKY: Ha! ha! (*all jump*) How dare you? Dat our queen,
unhand her.

ROB. C: What's sauce for goose is sauce for gander.

HOKY: You talk of sauce for goose, you'll find what dat is,
Dis old gal we shall dish up into patties.
And as for you.

SQUAW: Him under our protection.

HOKY: You are a – never mind – an interjection.

SQUAW: It shall not be, just keep your eyes on me,

And shortly you shall see what you shall see.

(*The Queen rushes off.*)

HOKY: What ho! there, call each culinary slavey,
          And served de couple hot with lots of gravy.

(*The cooks of* HOKY *enter with requisite cooking utensils, and prepare the fire for the feast.* ROB. C *and* MRS C *fall on their knees imploringly.*)

ROB. C: For once to your dread institute be undutiful,
          Remember we're so young.

MRS C: And we're so beautiful.

(*The* SQUAW *rushes on with her black amazons, who overpower the* KING'S *attendants.* ROB. C *and* MRS C *fall howling into each other's arms. They are torn asunder.*)

HOKY: What am de matter?

SQUAW: You're no longer King,
          We mean to rise and all that sort of thing.
          Behold my amazons, as each one fights,
          You'd better mind their lefts as well as rights.
          Cook him! At once her spouse the Queen deposes.
          Cook him at once.

HOKY: Cook me! Oh, jumping Moses!

(*The* SQUAW *carries off* ROB. C *followed by her amazons. The savages seize the* KING, *and carry him off with* MRS C. *Enter* ELF, *laughing.*)

ELF: Ha! ha! proud fairy, so you thought to keep
          This island to yourself, but I'm as deep
          As deep as Garrick as the saying is,
          And I can delve so low, or fly up fizz,
          Like a champagne cork up into the sky.
          The tricksiest of little elves am I.
          Talk of your Ariel, Puck, and such like spirits,
          Without the least detracting from their demerits,
          They're quite rococo, passe sort of fays
          In these express and big ballooning days,

When we e'en pierce the secrets of the sky,
So that we don't march with the times – we fly.

(*Enter* SEDATE FAIRY.)

S. FAIRY: That rascal Cupid really has upset us,
To think the squaw should fall into his fetters.
And that wretch Crusoe's married.

ELF: Ah, but we
Elves don't object much to polygamy
With human individuals like those,
It's what the French would call une autre chose,
Which when translated don't its sound much lose,
Une autre chose, 'another pair of shoes'.

S. FAIRY: I yet shall win the day, presumptuous elf.

ELF: I think my arts will triumph, ma'am, myself.

S. FAIRY: On their own merits modest elves are dumb.

ELF: But I'm an elf that isn't modest, mum,
But as they say in melo-drame 'they come'!

(S. FAIRY *and* ELF *retire to opposite sides. Enter* SQUAW *and*
CRUSOE.)

S. FAIRY Let's be invisible to mortal eyes
Just for a little, and their eyes surprise
With a remark or two.

ELF: All right, I'm game.
There! I'm invisible.

S. FAIRY There! I'm the same.

SQUAW: Oh, Crusoe, Crusoe, wherefore art thou, Crusoe?
I do so love you, Crusoe, which I do so.

ROB. C: As you love me, sweetest heart, I love you so.
'Tis true I have a wife.

SQUAW: You beauteous creature,
With true nobility in every feature;
E'en as you mention her the tear-drop trickles.
My love for you, sweet pale face, is all –

ELF: Pickles.

SQUAW (*offended*):   I wonder at it.

ROB. C: Love, I didn't speak.

S. FAIRY: You ought to be had up before the beak!

ROB. C (*to* SQUAW):   What do you mean by that?

SQUAW: Eh! mean by what?
Here comes my husband, followed by a lot
Of his late subjects. If we're caught – let's go.

(HOKY *rushes on, followed by savages*.)

HOKY: Mercy! keep off! I've never been your foe
Spare me, I'm old and tough! Oh, horror! horror!
Let me – oh let me – live until to-morrer.
See – see they collar me, they hold me tight,
And there the dreadful cauldron meets my sight,
In which, – oh, agony! – it can't be true –
You wouldn't of your monarch make a stew?
It's stew disgraceful. But behold the cook,
With flashing knife and fork, and furious look
Approaches. Don't! you can't, you shan't, you mustn't
Treat your great monarch like an old cock fuzzant,
Nor must you, least you'd suffer from remorse,
Serve him with your extremely ill-bred sauce.
Stand back! I am your king,

(*The savages, frightened, rush off*.)

They own my power.

(*turns, sees* ROB. C *and* SQUAW.,)

What do I see? The foreigner, the giaour,
The vile outside barbarian, the stranger!
And she – she smiles upon him! He's in danger!
I'll have his blood! I don't know what he got of it,
But whatsoe'er there is, I'll have the lot of it.
Intrusive party, die!

ROB. C: What would you do?

218

HOKY: Make mincemeat on dis berry spot of you.

(*The* KING *rushes with his dagger at* ROB. C, *and is about to dispatch him.* MRS C *rushes on, and interposes.*)

MRS C: Kill him, but first kill me.

HOKY: Me softened quite.

MRS C: Although the verdict would be 'sarve him right',
        We wives are so forgiving – he deserted,
        He left his wife and babbies, and he flirted
        Along with this black female, but I'm sure
        And he'll return.

ROB. C: Oh, won't he!

(*He rushes into* MRS C's *arms. The* ELF *and* S. FAIRY *come forward.*)

ELF: There you see,
        Men ain't so wicked as they seem to be.

S. FAIRY: Oh yes, they are, but really, Mrs C,
        Does quite surprise me, I give in.

ELF: You do?

S. FAIRY: I think I'll go in for a husband too.

ELF (*bowing*):   Hem! you don't say so, let me introduce,
        One who would –

S. FAIRY: Hold your tongue, you little goose,
        My scheme has failed.

HOKY (*who has been talking to* SQUAW):   You'll neber flirt no more?

MRS C (*to* ROB. C):   There's a big trading vessel near the shore,
        And you'll come home.

ROB. C: Rather.

MRS C: That will be splendid.

ELF: It seems, then, that our jolly row has ended.

S. FAIRY: Yes, I give in, I won't go on at men,
        Ever again.

ELF: I may come now and then?

S. FAIRY: Yes, now and then.

ELF: You fill me with delight.

           I'll pop in, then, and see you every night.

ELF: We to our several homes will go,
S. FAIRY: And not forget the past.

S. FAIRY: And let us hope our lessons will
           Prove lessons that will last.

SQUAW: Through trials and temptations we

MRS C: Triumphantly have gone.

HOKY: The King shall have his own again.

ROB. C: And she her Robinson!

(ROBINSON CRUSOE *embraces* MRS CRUSOE, HOKYPOKYWANKYFUM
embraces the SEDATE FAIRY *and* MAN FRIDAY *shakes hands with*
QUASHIBUNGO *as, for the last time, the curtain falls.*)

'Tis the Season
To be Jolly

Christmas Fun and Games

GAME, noun: Any unserious occupation designed for the relaxation of busy people and the distraction of idle ones; it's used to take people to whom we have nothing to say off our hands, and sometimes even ourselves. (Etienne Bonnot, *Dictionnaire des Synonymes.*)

As Mr Fezziwig in Dickens's *A Christmas Carol* remarked, of all the days in the year that we're familiar with, there's only one that's really fun – 25 December! So what better time to indulge in fun and games than at Christmas. In the pages that follow, there is a selection of Christmas entertainment that can be enjoyed by young and old alike and can ensure that your Christmas parties really go with a swing!

For all your games you might like to have a 'Lord of Misrule' too. In Scotland he is known as the Abbot of Unreason, but we like to call him the Lord of Misrule, a merrymaking anarchist who has been organizing party fun and games since the Ancient Romans played Pin the Laurel on the Caesar during the Saturnalia celebrations! The Lord of Misrule plans and masterminds all the games during a party, presents the prizes and hands out forfeits.

Children's Games

Santa Packed My Stocking
This is a word game that will make a welcome change after the boisterous antics of trying out all the new Christmas toys, and after two helpings of Christmas pudding, not to mention lashings of brandy butter, it will be a relief to sit down and play! Each player takes it in turn to list something that Santa put in their stocking, and as the game progresses, the list becomes longer and longer and l o n g e r. For example, the first player might say, 'Santa packed my stocking, and in it he put a model space shuttle.' The next player has to repeat what the first player said and add a present of his or her own, so it might be, 'Santa packed my stocking, and in it he put a model space shuttle and a wooden jigsaw.' Player number three adds another present, 'Santa packed my stocking, and in it he put a model space shuttle, a wooden jigsaw and three bananas.' The game goes on with each player adding an item. If anyone forgets a present or puts it in the wrong

order, he or she drops out. When there is one player left, he or she wins.

Watch the Whistle!

Before the game begins, a small plastic whistle should be prepared by attaching a short length of ribbon to it at the other end of which is a small safety pin. Everybody needs to be in on the secret of this game, except one poor unsuspecting person who is chosen to be the 'Lord of the Whistle'; his job is going to be to hunt the whistle and find it. If you have decided who is to be your 'Lord of Misrule' in this game he can perform a mock ceremony of knighting the 'Lord of the Whistle'.

Whilst the poor deluded player is kneeling down to be knighted, someone secretly pins the whistle carefully to the back of his jacket. The other players then pretend to pass the whistle amongst themselves, and make whistling sounds whenever the hunter's back is turned. Eventually he or she will cotton on to the fact that they have actually been in possession of the whistle all the time! Cruel, but fun!

Kim's Memory Game

Give each player a pencil and paper before you begin this game. You will then produce a tray on which have been set out twenty small objects. The players are allowed to study the tray's contents for just *one minute* and then the tray is covered with a cloth. The players must then write down on the paper as many of the objects as they can remember. The person who can remember the most is the winner. This game is loved by children and adults and is not as easy as it sounds. Here are some suggestions for possible objects that you could have on the tray:

1. A matchbox	11. A toy car
2. A pencil	12. A Christmas bauble
3. An eraser	13. An elastic band
4. A Scrabble letter	14. A comb
5. A watch	15. A cork
6. A teaspoon	16. A sugar lump
7. A candle	17. A cake decoration
8. A conker	18. A holly leaf
9. A playing card	19. A stamp
10. A button	20. An earring

Who's Who?

This is a good game to play if you have a lot of people in the room. You will need a large sheet or blanket. Send a player out of the room, and then hide one of the remaining people under the sheet. The player must then return and try to guess who it is. To make it a little more difficult, place a few cushions under the sheet as well! Another version of the game is to hide several players under the sheet with just their feet and ankles sticking out (remove their shoes and socks). The player must identify the people from their ankles!

Use Your Scents!

To set up the game the 'Lord of Misrule' must begin by exploring with his nose! Collect together ten different items that have a very distinctive smell and place each inside a matchbox that has a small hole punched in it. The players then have to sniff the boxes in turn and guess what is inside. The kitchen is a good place to find objects with a good aroma – spices like nutmeg and cinnamon, herbs such as thyme or a bayleaf, a lump of marzipan or almond paste, a slice of onion, and a clove of garlic are all excellent.

Falling Feather

Find a small, fluffy feather for this game. The players must sit in a tight circle on the floor, sitting as close together as possible. Someone holds the feather over the centre of the ring and lets it go. The players have to blow and flap their arms to keep the feather in the air for as long as possible, and if it falls on someone or touches them, that person must play a forfeit. It is as much fun watching people play this game as it is actually taking part!

Christmas Concert

All the players pretend that they are musicians in an orchestra and are each given a different instrument to 'play'. One is told that he is a violin, another a harp, one is a flute, a drum and so on until everyone has a different instrument on which to perform. The players must then imitate playing the instruments with actions and with their voice. The person leading the game chooses an instrument and begins to play a carol, the others all join in playing as loudly as they can. Each player must, however, keep an eye on the leading player for at any time and when least expected he or she will change instruments to one that somebody is already playing. The player who was playing that instrument must instantly change to the one the leader *was* playing. The players must be very alert and watch the leader's actions all the time.

Taboo

At any time over Christmas you can make one or two words totally taboo. For example, the words 'yes' and 'no', or even the word 'Christmas'. If anyone says the word they have to pay a forfeit. It sounds an easy game to play, but these little words soon slip out!

Shadow Buff

On one side of the room hang a white sheet, and behind it place a very bright lamp so that you produce a very large screen. All the rest of the lights are put out, and one at a time players go behind the screen and walk between the lamp and the sheet. Their shadow will come up on the screen but will often be very distorted, giving them the appearance of having a very long nose or chin. The other players have to guess who is behind the screen. To make the game more fun, hats, false noses and so on can be worn to make the disguise even more complete. The screen can also be used to cast all kinds of shadows on for players to guess. Impressions can be performed of famous people, or everyday objects can be held up to cast an unusual shadow. Alternatively, if someone is very clever with their hands, a simple shadow show can be performed, producing the images of rabbits, birds, dogs and so on. If no one can produce shadows with their hands, a good display can be made using silhouettes cut out of cardboard.

The Cushion Dance

This game is always fun for children to play, but give them plenty of room and move the Wedgwood and the Minton out of the way first. A cushion is placed on the floor in the middle of the room. The players link hands and form a circle around it, having first formed themselves into two equal teams, A and B. The players then dance around the cushion in a circle, but every now and again they must give a tug on the circle to try to get a player from the opposite team to touch the cushion with their foot. The player who steps on the cushion must leave the circle. The object is to force all the members of one team out. At the end of the game the team with players left in the circle are the winners, once all the opposers have been ejected.

The Picture Frame Game

To play this very amusing and entertaining game you will need a large picture frame. The empty frame is all you need, not one with a picture in it. The frame is given to the first player, who will hold it in front of his or her face and sit there with a completely straight unsmiling face. He must gaze through the frame for a full sixty seconds without flinching, giggling, grimacing, smirking, smiling or bursting into wild hysterical laughter. Easy, you may think, but at the same time all the rest of the players will be trying their hardest to raise a smile by pulling funny faces, doing silly walks, telling hilarious jokes, reciting rib-tickling poems, launching into loony limericks and generally trying to make him laugh. If the player manages to keep po-faced throughout, he or she deserves a prize! If not, the next player takes a turn at being framed.

Hot Boiled Beans and Bacon

One player is sent out of the room whilst a small object, such as a ring or thimble, is hidden. He is then given the invitation: 'Hot Boiled Beans and Bacon, make haste and come to supper.' The player begins to search the room for the hidden item, the other players will shout 'Very cold', 'cold', 'warmer', 'warm', 'hot', 'very hot' or 'burning', depending upon how close the person is to the hidden object.

Who Am I?

This is really a trick game and so the player who is to be the butt of the joke should be someone chosen with care, and not someone who is going to burst into tears, feel persecuted and have their Christmas ruined. A shy person is not going to enjoy playing this. Whoever you choose to play this is sent out of the room and told that while he is away the rest of the group are going to think of a famous person whom he must impersonate on his return. To help discover who that person is, he will be allowed to ask twenty questions, and when those twenty questions have been asked, he must then impersonate who he thinks the person is.

The secret is that when he has gone the group do not think of anyone at all, but agree to answer the victim's questions in a special way. If he asks a question that ends with a vowel, the answer will be 'Yes'. If the question ends with a consonant, the answer will be 'No', and whenever a question is asked that ends in a 'Y' the answer will be 'Yes and No'. The game could go like this:

'Am I someone who is British?'

'No.'

'Do I come from France?'

'Yes.'

'Am I male?'

'Yes.'

'Am I a character from history?'

'Yes and no!'

After twenty questions the poor victim will be thoroughly confused, and everyone else will be helpless with laughter. When they have been told what the real joke is, and assuming that they haven't walked out in disgust, the game can then be played for real. Alternatively another joke that can be played is to choose the person who has left the room to be the well-known person who is to be impersonated.

Pass the Balloon

This is another game that children love. Blow up a balloon so that it is as large as it will go without going off bang. Get the children to stand in a row one behind the other. Place the balloon between the knees of the first child and get them to turn round and, without letting the balloon fall to the ground, pass it on to the child behind. It must be passed all the way down the row without being touched by hand, and without being dropped. If it once touches the floor, it must go back to the first player again. If there are enough children taking part, divide them up into two teams. The first team to get their balloon from the front to the back of the row are the winners.

Christmas Raffle

This is a game that can be played by young and old alike, but children adore it. First get a number of little prizes, one for each child so that no one feels left out. Give each prize a number, and each child a ticket. Duplicates of the tickets can be dropped into a hat and then a local celebrity, such as Mum or Grandma, can be the one to dip into the hat and pick out the numbers. It is fun to have two hats, one for the children and one for the various prizes, so that holder of ticket number 2 perhaps wins prize number 7 and so on. If all prizes are of equal size and value, no child will feel hard done by and there will be no tears before bedtime!

Christmas Guessing Game

This takes a little preparation but is a good game for children at a party. The idea of the game is that you fill different containers with various objects, and the players have to guess how many are in each container. They keep a list of their guesses, and the player with the most correct answers is the winner. The game takes time to set up beforehand because you will have to do all the counting first to make sure that the answers are correct!

Here are some ideas for containers and things to put in them:

A box of walnuts – How many nuts?
A jam jar full of dried peas – How many peas?
A bottle full of coins – How many coins?
A plastic bag full of peanuts – How many peanuts?
A teapot packed with teabags – How many teabags?
A plastic bottle filled to a certain level with water – How much does it contain?
An exercise book – How many pages?
A length of ribbon – How long?
A branch of holly – How many berries?
A bottle of rubber bands – How many?

Playing Pairs

Take two packs of playing cards and spread them face down all over the floor. The players must sit around the edge of the cards in a large circle and take it in turns to pick up two cards. If the cards they pick up are a matching pair, either two kings, two aces, two threes, two jacks or whatever (they don't have to be the same suit), they keep the pair and have another go. If the two cards are different, they must be laid face downwards again, and the next player takes a turn.

The object of the game is to collect as many pairs as you can. The art of the game is to remember where certain cards have been laid. For example, you may have picked up a queen and an eight on your last go. Now this go you pick up an eight – and if only you can remember where you laid down the eight before, you will have a pair. It is important, and only fair, that each time you pick up a pair you let the other players see what you have picked up. The fun really begins when there are only a few cards left. Even with only four cards on the floor, it is still easy to pick up an odd pair and so let someone else win the game. An excellent game for improving your memory, and it's not only children who enjoy playing it.

Tricks and Illusions

However much fun playing games may be, it is always a good idea to have a short break to allow players to get their breath back and have another mince pie and a cup of Aunt Mildred's punch, before sharpening their wits for another round of Postman's Knock. There is no better diversion than a few conjuring tricks, well performed. The key to performing first-class tricks is PRACTICE. However simple a trick may appear, it needs to be rehearsed carefully so that it looks polished and you feel confident. Nothing would be more embarrassing than having to say 'Sorry, but that didn't quite work out.' The late, great Tommy Cooper made a career out of tricks going wrong, but it takes a first-rate magician to make illusions go wrong and appear funny, too. Read carefully a couple of times how each trick is done, and go through it step by step until you see how it works. When you can perform it in front of a mirror, with the book closed, and you feel happy doing it, Hey Presto! you are ready to put on a little Christmas extravaganza. Here are a few simple illusions mind-baffling to the uninitiated:

Mother Goose's Golden Egg
The Illusion: You take an ordinary hen's egg and challenge anyone to turn it into a golden egg. Before their very eyes you show them how it is done.
The Secret: On your table you will have a lighted candle. Hold the egg over the candle and turn it for a few seconds so that it becomes covered with soot and black. Drop the egg into a bowl of water and miraculously it will turn golden. The soot prevents the water from coming into contact with the egg and forms a surface a fractional distance away from the object which reflects the light with a metallic shine. Brilliant!

Christmas Money
The Illusion: You say that you are going to give the audience a chance to get back some of the money they have spent over Christmas. You take six ordinary envelopes and say that one of them contains a £5 note. You then invite five people to choose an envelope and leave one remaining. They can shuffle the envelopes

as much as they like and take the one they have chosen back to their seat. Ask them not to feel the envelopes as they choose them as this would be unfair. When they get back to their seats, they can open up the envelopes and inside will discover a piece of paper bearing the words: 'SORRY! THIS IS NOT A £5 NOTE.' You take the last envelope, and inside is a £5 note!

The Secret: The six envelopes are all arranged on a tray or plate. Underneath the tray and held in place by your fingers is the £5 note.

After the people have taken off their envelopes, push the remaining one under your thumb while they are opening theirs. When you take the envelope off the tray, slide the note off with it. Open the envelope with your other hand and pretend to take out the note. Practise this carefully so that it looks as if you really do take the note out of the envelope.

Who's a Nana?

The Illusion: Take a bunch of bananas and say that you are fed up with the conventional method of peeling and eating bananas and that you have invented a new way. You say that it's easy to get a banana to slice itself. Waving your hand over a banana, you unpeel it to reveal it already cut into slices. But, you continue, it's not so easy to get a banana to peel itself. You chop the end off a banana, put it in the neck of a bottle and the banana mysteriously sheds its skin and pops out into the bottle.

The Secret: For the sliced banana, simply insert a needle into a banana at various points and push it from side to side so that it slices the fruit up. The skin remains intact and the pinholes won't be seen, but the banana will be mysteriously cut up when you unpeel it.

For the other illusion, take a bottle and put about a teaspoon of methylated spirits in the bottom. Drop a lighted match into the bottle and then chop the end off your banana. As the flames die down, insert the prepared end of the fruit into the neck of the bottle and to the amazement of all, the banana will be mysteriously sucked inside, because the air inside the bottle contracts to form a vacuum.

Card Reading

The Illusion: No, not Christmas card reading, but playing-card reading! You begin this trick by blindfolding yourself with a scarf.

You then take a pack of cards and hold them so that they are all facing towards the audience. You then proceed to go through the pack, naming every single card even though you are blindfolded and the cards are not facing you.

The Secret: As with all great illusions, you CHEAT! The first cheat is that you tie the blindfold on yourself, not allowing a member of the audience to do it for you, and you tie it so that you can just see under the bottom of the blindfold.

The second cheat is the manner in which you show the cards to your audience. Before you start, you hold the pack of cards face downwards and turn the top card face upwards. When you hold the pack up to face the audience, have this card facing them. They will automatically assume that this is the bottom of the pack and that all the cards are facing the same way. As they are looking at the card, you name it for them, at the same time noting the card that is facing you by peeping under the blindfold.

When you have named the first card, put the pack behind your back and transfer the card you have just noted to the audience side of the pack. Show the pack to the audience, naming the card they can now see. Continue doing this throughout the whole pack. You will know when you have done this because you will reach the back of a card, the first card that was originally facing the audience.

The trick can actually appear quite amazing when performed without a blindfold, but a blindfold makes it just that little bit more spectacular. To baffle the audience even further, you can get one of them to shuffle the pack before you begin so that they know you haven't simply learnt the order in which the cards appear.

Magic Water

The Illusion: For this you have one empty glass, a tumbler of water and a handkerchief. You tell the audience that the water you have in the tumbler, although it looks quite ordinary, is in fact magic water. The water has incredible powers and you can pour it into the glass and place a handkerchief over the top, and when you turn the glass upside-down, no water will fall out. This you do, and then – to astound your audience to tally – you command the water to bubble and boil, and before long they see the water apparently boiling!

The Secret: When you fill up the glass with water, you should fill it to only about three-quarters full. When you cover the glass with the handkerchief, pick it up with your right hand, and with your left hand draw the handkerchief's edges under the bottom of the glass. Hold the bottom of the glass and the handkerchief with your left hand and press down the centre of the handkerchief with your right hand until it just, but only just, touches the water. Then, with a sharp twist of the wrist, turn the tumbler over. Don't worry, no water will spill out!

Still holding the glass upside-down, draw the handkerchief tighter around the glass until the concave shape going into the glass becomes taut across the rim. The water will now drop to this level (but no further), and a vacuum will have been created at the bottom of the glass. Gradually air will penetrate through the handkerchief and travel through the water to fill the vacuum at the bottom of the glass, causing the water to bubble and so look and sound as if it is boiling.

Practise this illusion over a bowl or bath until you are confident about performing it.

Clairvoyance

The Illusion: On a cold crisp Christmas evening, the atmosphere is right for a little clairvoyance, but to retain peace and goodwill, we will deal with the living and not the dead! You, as the clairvoyant, are blindfolded by a member of the audience, and the blindfold is tied tightly and covers your eyes totally so that everyone knows that you cannot see anything, and you really can't. Your assistant for this illusion will then ask a member of the audience to go and touch a certain object in the room, quietly. A dialogue such as this will then proceed between you and your assistant:

'Do you remember how this room is furnished in which we are sitting?'

'Yes.'

'Do you remember the colour of the curtains?'

'Yes.'

'Do you know the books on the bookshelf?'

'Yes.'

'And the porcelain figure on top?'

'Yes.'

'Do you remember the china in the cabinet?'

'Yes.'

'The painting above the fireplace?'

'Yes.'

'You think there is nothing in this room that has escaped your notice?'

'Nothing.'

'All right. You cannot possibly have seen where Marjorie (the member of the audience) went to in this room of her own free will. Can you tell us what she is now holding?'

'The porcelain figure on top of the bookcase.'

'Correct!'

The Secret: The porcelain figure was the only object preceded by the word 'And', which is what you, the clairvoyant, will listen for and is the signal given by the assistant when stating what is being touched. A simple piece of trickery, but it fools the audience every time.

A more detailed act of this nature can be developed with a lot of pre-arranged signals. The assistant can go among the audience and hold up personal items for the clairvoyant to say what they are:

If it is a watch – '*What* is this I am holding?'

If a ring – '*Let* us know what this is.'

If a brooch – '*Now* what am I holding?'

If a cuff-link – 'Say *exactly* what I am holding' – and so on.

Magic Christmas Card

The Illusion: You hold up an ordinary Christmas card and a pair of scissors, and challenge anyone in the audience to cut a hole large enough to climb through. It is unlikely that anyone will rise to the challenge, and even if they do, it is doubtful whether they will succeed. You then take the card, cut a hole in it and proceed to climb right through.

The Secret: This lies in the way in which you cut the card. Make a slit along the spine of the card, like this:

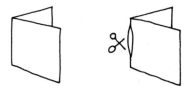

Next make a series of cuts across the card, through both thicknesses. The first cut should run along the spine to a centimetre from the edge of the card, then you make another and another until you have six cuts:

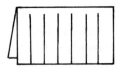

Now turn the card the other way and make six similar cuts, once again about a centimetre from the edge:

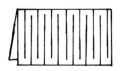

When you open the card, you will discover that you have a giant loop which will now be big enough for you to climb right through. This illusion fascinates children and is something they can learn to do themselves.

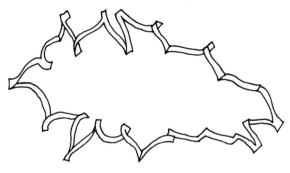

Your Number's Up!
The Illusion: Take a blank sheet of paper and tell the audience that you are going to write a number on it. This you do. You then fold the paper in half, place it in an envelope and seal it down. You then place the envelope on a table in full view of the audience where they can see that it is not touched again or tampered with.

Next you take a second sheet of paper and announce that you are going to write down three numbers. Your conversation will probably be something like this:

'I'd like someone to tell me their date of birth. In which year were you born, sir?'

'1965.'

'1965 – good. I've written that down. Now under that I would like to put a famous historical date. Can you think of one, madam?'

'1066.'

'1066 – super. I've written that underneath 1965. Now, just to make the trick even trickier, I'm going to ask someone to write down a third number underneath the first two, without telling me what the third number is. Will you do this for me, sir?'

Having got three numbers like this, you then ask someone to add them up and tell you what the total is. In this example the total is 4,142. Finally you ask someone to step forward and take your original envelope off the table and open it. Inside they will find a piece of paper on which you have written a number. The number on the paper will, of course, be 4,142.

The Secret: The envelope inside which you have written a number remains in full view of the audience throughout the trick, and yet you cannot possibly know which numbers are going to be given to you beforehand.

Magic? Not really! The secret is that you have a helper in the audience, and he or she is the one that writes down the third number for you. Before you begin, he or she will know which number you have written in the envelope. It can be any number, but must be over 4,000. The job of the helper is to write down a number which, when added to the first two given by genuine members of the audience, will give the number you want.

Your assistant will need to be good at arithmetic, because he will need to do the calculation quickly in his head. As you pass him the piece of paper with 1965 and 1066 on it, he must mentally add those two together ($1,965 + 1,066 = 3,031$) and then take away the number for the answer you want ($4,142 = 3,031 + 1,111$) to get the number that he will need to write down. He will then pass the paper on to someone else to add up, who will come up with the number written inside the envelope.

Adult Games

No, forget the steamy XXX-rated antics. Adults love playing games just as much as, if not more than, children do! Here are some that no Christmas party should be without.

Lovers

A real getting-to-know-you game if your party consists of people who haven't met before. On pieces of card write down the names of great lovers, Anthony and Cleopatra, Romeo and Juliet, Kermit and Miss Piggy, Prince Albert and Queen Victoria, and so on, and give everybody a card with a name on as they arrive. By mingling with the other guests they must subtly discover who their 'lover' is. If there are more women than men, give a man 'Henry VIII' and six women the names of his wives!

The Matchbox Game

Once all your guests have got to know each other's names, you can play something more intimate – yes, the matchbox game! Divide the players into two teams, each team standing in a straight line. The person at the head of each team pushes a matchbox cover on his nose and on the word 'go' turns to the next person in the team and attempts to transfer the matchbox onto his or her nose. No hands are allowed and the first team to transfer their matchbox nose-by-nose from one end of the team to the other is the winner. Be fair when picking the teams, and don't give one side all the big noses!

Dumb Crambo

Divide the players into two teams and send one team out of the room. The team remaining have to think of a verb for the other team to guess. When it has been chosen, the other team can come in and are told a word that the verb rhymes with. The team are allowed to confer and then silently mime what they think the verb is. For example, they could have been told that it rhymes with BUY. They might think the verb is TIE, and begin miming tying up a parcel. If they are wrong, the other team will hiss loudly and they will have to think again. If they mime the verb FLY and are correct, the other team will applaud and then take their turn at guessing a verb.

Up The Stairs

For a quieter and more relaxing game, players can be given a sheet of paper and a pencil and are given any letter of the alphabet and have to work out a word staircase like this, with words going across:

A

A T

A N T

A U N T

A N K L E

A N T L E R

A N O T H E R

A S S A S S I N

A T R O C I O U S

A S P I R A T I ON

A S S I G N A T I ON

A C A N T H A C E O U S

A C C E L O R O M E T E R

A C C O M P L I S H M E N T

A C K N O W L E D G E M E N T

A C A N T H O P T E R Y G I A N

A E R O T H E R M O D Y N A M I C

A N T I F E R R O M A G N E T I S M

A D R E N O L O R T I C O T R O P I C

Most people should be able to get up to ten letters, but the cleverer people may get much longer. Dictionaries can be allowed if players feel that their intelligence is threatened! The game can be played working your way through the letters of the alphabet.

Knees Up

A lighter game that always causes a giggle but is best played amongst couples who know each other well. All the females are sent out of the room, and their husbands or lovers roll up their trousers exposing their knees. The women are blindfolded one at a time and have to feel each of the knees in turn to guess which belongs to their husband or lover. This can be hilarious, especially if another man not connected with any of the women is substituted for someone's partner!

Adverbs

Not as intellectual as it sounds! (An adverb is a 'describing' word, for those that do not know.) A player is sent out of the room while the rest of the players choose an adverb. When the outsider returns, he has to guess that adverb and can ask any player to perform some task or action in the manner of the adverb. The adverb might be something like 'sexily' or 'solemnly', 'sadly', 'boisterously', 'jauntily' – and the player can ask someone to perform an action in that manner – walking, knitting, reading, dancing, eating and so on. When he has seen several different actions done in a particular manner, he can attempt to guess what the adverb is.

Obviously some adverbs are much harder to guess (and perform) than others. To do something 'furtively' is harder to guess than something done 'merrily', so choose adverbs to suit the intelligence of the players.

The Minister's Cat

If you've invited the vicar round for a Christmas sherry, this is a good game to play. All the players can sit in a circle, and the first player says: 'The Minister's cat was an Artful cat.' The next player says: 'The Minister's cat was an Artistic cat.' So the game continues until everyone has come up with a word beginning with 'A' to describe the cat. Then you move on to the letter 'B' for 'The Minister's cat is a Bumptious cat.' Work through the letters of the alphabet, although it will get more difficult as you go along, but you can have Xenophobic cats and Zealous cats!

A much more difficult version is to use different members of the clergy too. For example, 'The Archbishop's cat is an Atrocious cat,' 'The Bishop's cat is a Boring cat,' 'The Curate's cat is a Calculating cat,' 'The Dean's cat is a Domineering cat,' and so on.
For yet another version, give the cats names, like this:
'The Minister's cat is a Funny cat and his name is Fred.'
'The Minister's cat is a Glorious cat and his name is Gilbert.'
'The Minister's cat is a Heavy cat and his name is Henry.'
'The Minister's cat is an Ironical cat and his name is Idris.'
'The Minister's cat is a Jovial cat and his name is Jonathan.'

Charades
No Christmas party could possibly be complete without the best loved of all Christmas games, charades. Divide the players into groups of two or four and get each one to think of a 'charade'. It will be a word, a phrase, the title of a book, play, film or song, TV or radio programme and the team must act it out, syllable by syllable or part by part, in a series of silent but inventive mimes. Each team takes it in turn to perform, and the rest have to guess the word, phrase or title in question.

To help the spectators, the leader of each team is allowed to say whether it is a single word, phrase or title and how many words it contains. After that, the performers must keep completely silent. To get you going, here are a few words that lend themselves to the playing of charades, with ideas for how the syllables might be mimed in brackets:
Airline (air/line)
Ambulance (Am/boo/lance)
Artichoke (Art/tea/choke)
Brassière (Brass/sea/air)
Bystander (Buy/stand/err)
Carpet (Car/pet)
Capitalize (Cap/it/all/eyes)
Dandelion (Dandy/lion)
Dialogue (Die/a/log)
Dinosaur (Die/no/saw)
Earnest (Her/nest)
Engrave (Hen/grave)
Farcical (Far/cycle)
Fortunate (Four/tune/ate)

Gastric (Gas/trick)
Hospital (Horse/spit/all)
Indignation (Inn/dig/nation)
Kingfisher (King/fisher)
Literature (Litter/rat/ewer)
Mathematics (Moth/her/Mat/ticks)
Naughtiness (Nought/tea/Ness)
Orangeade (Or/range/aid)
Punctuality (Puncture/all/high/tea)
Rumbustious (Rum/bust/tea/us)
Selfish (Sell/fish)
Trampoline (Tramp/hole/lean)
Utensil (You/tense/ill)
Vanguard (Van/guard)
Wigwam (Wig/wham)

Here are some possible titles:

The Wind in the Willows
A Christmas Carol
This Is Your Life
A Little Night Music
Cats
Gone With the Wind

When each syllable in a word or each word in a title has been performed, the word or title as a whole must be given.

More Famous Than Botticelli

This favourite Victorian game is still very popular at Christmas and can be played by as few as two people but is better with a large number.

The object of the game is for one person to think of someone (more famous than Botticelli!), and the other players have to ask questions to find out that person's identity. For example, the famous English navigator Captain Cook might be chosen. The game might go like this:

'Is the person living or dead?'
'Dead.'
'Is it male or female?'
'Male.'
'Is it someone from fact or fiction?'
'Fact.'

240

'Was he a politician?'
'No.'
'Was he an actor?'
'No.'
'Was he an explorer?'
'Yes.'
'Was he a sailor?'
'Yes.'
'Is it Christopher Columbus?'
'No.'
And so the game continues, with players taking it in turns to find out the person's identity.

Happy Christmas!
This is a game that players of all ages can take part in, providing they are numerate. Players take it in turns to count from one to infinity, with each player saying a different number, but the numbers five and seven (and multiples of five and seven) must never be mentioned. Instead, when you get a five or a multiple of five, you say 'Happy Christmas', and when you get a seven or a multiple of seven you say 'Happy New Year'. When you get to a number that is a multiple of five and seven, you say 'Happy Christmas and a Happy New Year'. Here's how it goes from one to ten:
One
Two
Three
Four
HAPPY CHRISTMAS
Six
HAPPY NEW YEAR
Eight
Nine
HAPPY CHRISTMAS
Anyone caught saying the winning number has to pay a forfeit. The last one left counting is the winner.

Forfeits
An evening playing games without forfeits would certainly be incomplete, and often watching forfeits is greater fun than playing

the actual game. Here is a list of forfeits which can be written on to cards and drawn out by a losing player:

1. Laugh in the corner of one room, sing in another, cry in another, and dance in another.

2. Kiss the person you love best in the room. (This can be got round by kissing everyone!)

3. Leave the room with two legs and come back with six. (Bring a chair in with you!)

4. Spelling backwards. (The player must be made to spell a long word, like 'hydrostatics' backwards.)

5. Kneel to the wittiest, bow to the prettiest, and kiss the one you love best.

6. Kiss your own shadow. (Stand with the light behind you so that it casts a shadow on someone's face!)

7. Be a statue. (The person must stand perfectly still until told that he can stop. Don't leave him too long!)

8 Be the Opposite. (Whatever players tell him to do, he must do the contrary.)

9. Act the Parrot. (Players can say ridiculous things which the one paying the forfeit must repeat like a parrot.)

10. Make a short speech without once using the letter 'L'.

Christmas Aftermath

All good things must come to an end, and on Twelfth Night the Christmas season ends for yet another year. As the remaining plum pudding is fried in butter, the turkey minced into rissoles, the last drop of punch drained, the Yule candles are blown out for the last time, the cards come down and the decorations are packed away, there are a few points to remember that will help make life easier *next* Christmas.

Decorations
Pack them all together carefully in a large cardboard box, together with the drawing-pins that kept them in place. Wind tinsel into a ball, pack baubles into tissue, and sellotape the box down and mark in large letters 'CHRISTMAS DECORATIONS'. If you keep your Christmas candles and everything necessary, you will find that, if you keep the box tucked safely away in the attic, everything will be together when next you want it.

Fairy Lights
Check these carefully before you pack them away. Make sure that

all the bulbs are screwed in tightly, that any broken bulbs have been replaced and that none of the cable or wires has been inadvertently damaged or frayed. If you no longer have the box in which they came, wind the lights around a strip of cardboard to prevent their becoming a tangled mess, and they should be in perfect working order next Christmas.

Holly, Ivy and Mistletoe
When you take down your Christmas plants and decorations, don't throw them away. Take off the best leaves and press and dry them. If you keep them carefully in sealed polythene bags when *completely* dry, you can use them next year for making Christmas cards and collages next year.

Christmas Paper
On Christmas Day, when presents are unwrapped, to save being buried under a mound of paper take a large plastic sack and, as the gifts are unwrapped, put the torn and unusable rubbish straight into the sack, which can then easily be disposed of. Keep your eyes open for good pieces of paper, ribbon etc. and keep them to one side. Take a long cardboard roll from the centre of kitchen foil and roll the paper around it. You can put as many layers around the roll as you like and then keep it in position with a rubber band. The paper will keep perfectly.

Christmas Cards
Unfortunately, without your appearing like Scrooge, old Christmas cards cannot be used again – not as Christmas cards anyway. You can, however, cut them up to make small gift tags for presents. Many charities advertise for cards after Christmas, and it is a very worthwhile method of disposing of them, but if you can't find a charity that wants them, contact a local infant or primary school, who can often find use for them. As a final resort, cut them up and use them for scrap paper.

Unwanted Presents
Any unwanted gifts that you may have can be given to any charity shop or Senior Citizens' home, where they will be put to good use.

Christmas Trees
If you have bought a tree with roots, plant it in the garden or in a small tub. If in a tub, it can be used for years to come. If you

happened to buy one without roots that will die, gather the pine needles and crush them. Boil with some pure vegetables or corn oil and a tablespoon of vodka to make a pine essence.

Card/Present Lists

Make sure you have marked off all those from whom you have received cards and presents, and keep the list somewhere safe, preferably in your box of decorations so that you know exactly where to lay your hands on it next December. Keep together any carol song sheets, Yuletide recipes and anything else that comes into use just once a year. After all, there are fewer than 350 days left till Christmas!

Bibliography

Book of Household Management, Mrs Beeton (1859)

Seven Centuries of English Cooking, M. McKendry

The History of the Christmas Card, George Buday (Spring Books, 1954)

Traditional British Cookery, Maggie Malpas Pearce (David & Charles, 1972)

Cooking for Christmas, Audrey Parker (Faber & Faber, 1972)

Discovering Pantomime, Gyles Brandreth (Shire Publications, 1973)

I Scream for Ice-Cream: Pearls from the Pantomime, Gyles Brandreth (Eyre Methuen, 1974)

Food by Appointment, Michele Brown (Elm Tree Books, 1977)

The Complete Home Entertainer, Gyles Brandreth (Robert Hale, 1981)

Everyman's Indoor Games, Gyles Brandreth (Dent, 1982)

Index